CARCASSONNE TRAVEL GUIDE 2025 & 2026

Explore the Legendary Walled Fortress City in the South of France with Insider Tips and Easy Itineraries for an Unforgettable Journey

Lina Rocca

About The Author

lina rocca is a wanderer at heart and a storyteller by nature. She doesn't just travel, she dives headfirst into the unknown, turning every trip into a story worth telling. Her guides aren't just pages of facts; they're invitations to experience places with fresh eyes and an open heart.

With Lina, it's all about discovering the hidden alleys, the local flavors, the moments others might miss. Her writing is a warm conversation, full of practical tips but also sprinkled with the kind of personal insights that make you feel like you're exploring with a friend.

Whether you're chasing off-the-beaten-path adventures or simply want to get the most out of your next city break, lina rocca's guides help you do just that. They're about making travel effortless, enjoyable, and deeply memorable because for Lina, every journey is a chance to learn, connect, and grow.

If you're ready to see the world beyond the usual sights, lina rocca is the perfect companion to show you the way.

TABLE OF CONTENTS

INTRODUCTION   **7**

    Welcome to the Walled Wonder of France   7

    A Brief History of Carcassonne   11

    Why Visit Carcassonne in 2025 & 2026   15

CHAPTER 1   **20**

PLANNING YOUR TRIP   **20**

    Best Times to Visit Carcassonne   20

    How to Get to Carcassonne   24

    Budgeting and Currency Tips   28

CHAPTER 2   **33**

GETTING AROUND CARCASSONNE   **33**

    Walking the Medieval Streets   33

    Public Transport and Bike Rentals   37

    Accessibility and Navigation Tips   41

CHAPTER 3   **46**

WHERE TO STAY   **46**

    Best Areas for First-Time Visitors   46

    Boutique Hotels and Charming Guesthouses
    50

    Family-Friendly and Budget
    Accommodations   54

CHAPTER 4   **59**

WHAT TO EAT AND DRINK   **59**

    Traditional Languedoc Cuisine   59

    Best Restaurants, Cafés, and Markets   64

    Local Wines and Regional Specialties   68

CHAPTER 5   **74**

CULTURE AND TRADITIONS   **74**

     Festivals and Annual Events   74

     Language, Customs, and Etiquette   79

     Art, Music, and Local Handicrafts   83

CHAPTER 6   **89**

LANDMARKS AND MUST-SEE ATTRACTIONS   **89**

     Cité de Carcassonne: The Walled Fortress 89

     Château Comtal and Ramparts Walk   94

     Basilica of Saints Nazarius and Celsus   98

     Bastide Saint-Louis: The Lower Town   102

CHAPTER 7   **107**

OUTDOOR ADVENTURES   **107**

     Walking and Cycling the Canal du Midi   107

     Wine Tours and Vineyard Excursions   111

     Day Trips to the Pyrenees and Cathar Castles   116

CHAPTER 8   **121**

SMART TRAVEL TIPS   **121**

     Safety and Health Essentials   121

     Packing Tips and Local Etiquette   126

     Useful Apps and Emergency Contacts   130

CHAPTER 9   **135**

SAMPLE ITINERARIES   **135**

     One Day in Carcassonne: Highlights Tour 135

     Three-Day Itinerary: History, Food &

Culture   139
A Week in Carcassonne and Beyond   144
CONCLUSION   **149**
Final Thoughts and Inspiration for Your
Journey   149

Languedoc-Roussillon

MENDE

FLORAC

ALES

LE VIGAN

NIMES

LODEVE

MONTPELLIER

BEZIERS

NARBONNE

CARCASSONNE

LIMOUX

PERPIGNAN

PRADES

CERET

INTRODUCTION

<u>Welcome to the Walled Wonder of France</u>

Welcome to Carcassonne, a medieval masterpiece nestled in the heart of the Languedoc region in southern France. With its fairy-tale turrets, double rings of stone walls, and cobbled streets steeped in centuries of history, Carcassonne is not merely a destination, it is an experience, a journey back in time that will awaken your imagination and leave a lasting impression on your soul. As you step into this UNESCO World Heritage Site, you'll quickly understand why Carcassonne is often described as one of the most enchanting fortified cities in Europe.

Carcassonne is a city where the past and present coexist harmoniously. Its most iconic feature, the Cité de Carcassonne, dominates the skyline with its imposing battlements and storybook towers. Walking through its arched gates is like opening a portal to the Middle Ages, where every stone whispers tales of knights, crusaders, and royal intrigue. But Carcassonne is not just about its legendary fortress. Beyond the citadel lies a vibrant lower town, known as the Bastide Saint-Louis, filled with charming shops, cozy cafés, colorful markets, and warm-hearted locals who embody the spirit of southern France.

This travel guide is designed to be your trusted companion as you uncover the secrets of Carcassonne in 2025 and 2026. Whether you are planning a quick getaway or a leisurely holiday, you'll find everything you need in the following pages from practical travel tips and cultural insights to must-see landmarks, local gastronomy, and carefully crafted itineraries. But most importantly, this guide aims to help you truly connect with Carcassonne, beyond just its picture-perfect views. It invites you to immerse yourself in the rhythms of local life, to listen to the echoes of the past in every stone wall and chapel, and to let the town's enduring beauty inspire your own personal journey.

What sets Carcassonne apart from other medieval towns is the astonishing scale and preservation of its ancient fortress. The walled Cité includes 52 towers and nearly 3 kilometers of defensive ramparts that create a dramatic silhouette against the southern French sky. Once a critical stronghold during the Albigensian Crusade in the 13th century, Carcassonne has seen centuries of sieges, restoration efforts, and cultural evolution. Its storied history is matched only by its architectural grandeur. The Cité is a living museum, yet far from static it is alive with restaurants, artisan boutiques, street performers, and festivals that bring its storied walls to life throughout the year.

But Carcassonne is more than just history. It is a gateway to the beauty and diversity of the Occitanie region. Nearby you'll find the tranquil waters of the Canal du Midi, the scenic vineyards that produce the robust wines of Corbières and Minervois, and a patchwork of countryside trails perfect for hiking, biking, or day trips into the Pyrenees. The local culture is a proud blend of Occitan heritage and modern French flair. Here, time moves a bit more slowly, meals are savored more deeply, and hospitality is offered with genuine warmth.

Whether you're a solo traveler in search of architectural splendor, a couple looking for a romantic escape, a history buff yearning to explore medieval battlements, or a family ready to introduce children to the magic of old-world France,

Carcassonne offers something special. The years 2025 and 2026 are particularly promising times to visit. With travel momentum building again, but crowds still manageable, you'll have the rare opportunity to experience this timeless destination with the space and serenity it deserves.

In this guide, you'll learn how to plan your visit to Carcassonne efficiently and enjoyably, with insights into the best times to go, how to get there, and where to stay. You'll be introduced to the city's most celebrated landmarks, from the majestic Château Comtal to the sacred Basilica of Saints Nazarius and Celsus. You'll discover the unique flavors of Languedoc cuisine, from cassoulet to locally grown olives and robust reds. You'll be invited to participate in cultural traditions and festivals that breathe life into Carcassonne's cobbled lanes. And most importantly, you'll be empowered to travel smartly and sustainably, making the most of your adventure while respecting the town's rich heritage and delicate charm.

So take a deep breath, let go of the fast pace of modern life, and get ready to step into a world of wonder. Carcassonne awaits you not as a relic of the past, but as a living, breathing town that continues to inspire travelers just like you. Let this be the beginning of a journey that brings not only memories and photographs, but a renewed sense of connection to the timeless stories of humanity, and to the enduring beauty of one of France's most unforgettable destinations.

A Brief History of Carcassonne

Carcassonne's story stretches back over two millennia, weaving together layers of history that are still visible in its streets, towers, and walls today. From its humble origins as a pre-Roman settlement to its development as a medieval stronghold and eventual recognition as a UNESCO World Heritage Site, Carcassonne has played many roles throughout history, each one adding to its rich tapestry of culture and legacy.

The earliest traces of settlement in Carcassonne date back to around 3,500 years ago, when the hilltop location where the Cité now stands was chosen for its strategic advantages. During the 6th century BCE, the area was settled by the Iberians and later by the Romans, who fortified it into an important outpost known as "Carcaso." Under Roman rule, the town developed rapidly, with roads, baths, and a fortified wall that provided protection and established Carcassonne as a key military and trading hub in the region.

As the Roman Empire waned, Carcassonne's importance only grew. In the 5th century, it was conquered by the Visigoths, who further strengthened the city's defenses. These early fortifications laid the foundation for what would become one of the most formidable medieval strongholds in Europe. During this period, the fortress town became a center of political power and military strategy, marking Carcassonne's transformation from Roman outpost to medieval bastion.

In the 8th century, Carcassonne briefly fell under the control of the Saracens Muslim forces from the Iberian Peninsula before being reclaimed by Frankish forces under Charles Martel. The city's name is often linked to a legend from this era: the tale of Lady Carcas. According to the story, she tricked the besieging army into believing the town was well-stocked by tossing a well-fed pig over the walls, leading them to abandon their siege. When the bells rang in celebration, the phrase "Carcas sonne" ("Carcas rings") was said to have given the city its name. Though apocryphal, this legend remains part of local folklore and contributes to Carcassonne's mystical allure.

By the 12th century, Carcassonne had become a prosperous and autonomous city ruled by the powerful Trencavel family. However, its fortunes changed dramatically in the early 13th century during the Albigensian Crusade, a brutal military campaign initiated by the Catholic Church to eliminate the Cathar heresy in southern France. Carcassonne, known for its Cathar sympathies, was besieged and captured in 1209 by crusader forces led by Simon de Montfort. The Trencavel ruler was imprisoned and later died in captivity, and the city was annexed into the French crown's territories.

Following the Crusade, Carcassonne was heavily fortified under royal command. The Château Comtal (Count's Castle) was constructed within the inner walls, and the city became a key part of France's frontier defenses against the Kingdom of Aragon. The iconic double walls and 52 watchtowers that define the Cité's silhouette were largely built during the 13th and 14th centuries. These massive defenses made Carcassonne one of the most secure cities of its time and a symbol of royal power and military architecture.

As the political landscape of Europe changed and national borders stabilized, Carcassonne gradually lost its military importance. By the 17th century, its fortifications were considered obsolete, and the town's prominence declined. The lower town, known as the Bastide Saint-Louis, became the commercial center, while the old Cité fell into disrepair.

In the 19th century, Carcassonne faced a turning point. The French government considered demolishing the crumbling fortress, but a passionate campaign led by historian Jean-Pierre Cros-Mayrevieille and architect Eugène Viollet-le-Duc succeeded in preserving and restoring the Cité. Viollet-le-Duc's ambitious restoration project, although sometimes controversial for its romanticized interpretation of medieval architecture, saved Carcassonne from ruin and gave the fortress its current appearance. His work included rebuilding the towers with conical slate roofs, reconstructing walls, and revitalizing key structures like the Château Comtal and Basilica of Saints Nazarius and Celsus.

In 1997, the historic Cité of Carcassonne was officially designated a UNESCO World Heritage Site, cementing its global recognition as a cultural treasure. Today, Carcassonne stands as a rare example of a complete and intact fortified medieval city, drawing visitors from around the world who come to admire its preservation and walk the same paths once trodden by soldiers, merchants, pilgrims, and kings.

Understanding Carcassonne's history is key to appreciating its spirit. Every corner of the city tells a story from the worn stone steps of its ramparts to the echoes in its Gothic chapels. It is a place where ancient legends, historical drama, and architectural splendor converge to create a living monument to the past. As you explore its streets and landmarks, you are not just sightseeing, you are walking through the chapters of a fascinating historical saga that continues to shape the identity of Carcassonne to this day.

Why Visit Carcassonne in 2025 & 2026

There has never been a better time to plan a trip to Carcassonne than in 2025 and 2026. With its captivating blend of medieval grandeur, cultural richness, and contemporary charm, Carcassonne offers a travel experience that feels both timeless and refreshingly new. These years present a unique window of opportunity for travelers to witness the city at its very best, less crowded than major tourist centers, but alive with local events, seasonal festivals, and fresh opportunities for exploration. Whether you're a seasoned globetrotter or a curious first-time visitor, Carcassonne promises a journey that is as immersive as it is unforgettable.

One of the most compelling reasons to visit in 2025 and 2026 is the continued resurgence of mindful travel. Post-pandemic tourism has shifted in tone; travelers now seek deeper, more meaningful connections with the places they visit. Carcassonne, with its strong historical identity and manageable scale, is perfectly suited to this renewed focus on authenticity and cultural engagement. You won't find overwhelming crowds or manufactured experiences here. Instead, you'll discover a city that invites you to slow down, walk its cobbled alleys, speak with artisans, and absorb centuries of history at your own pace.

In 2025 and 2026, Carcassonne is expected to host an expanded calendar of cultural events that make the most of its legendary setting. Each summer, the Festival de Carcassonne transforms the town into a grand open-air stage, with dozens of performances ranging from classical music and opera to rock concerts and theater productions. These upcoming editions promise to be some of the most dynamic yet, with international artists joining local talent to create a festival atmosphere that spreads from the Cité to the Bastide. Additionally, medieval fairs, artisan markets, and food festivals ensure that visitors at any time of the year can enjoy the vibrant life of the region.

For those interested in historical travel, Carcassonne offers a pristine and richly preserved medieval environment that is unlike anything else in Europe. The double-walled Cité, complete with drawbridges, towers, and narrow stone passageways, gives visitors the rare chance to walk through a city that looks almost exactly as it did hundreds of years ago. With fewer tourists in these transitional years compared to pre-2020 levels, visitors in 2025 and 2026 can experience these iconic sites with a sense of calm and space—ideal for photography, reflection, and uninterrupted exploration.

Travel infrastructure is also improving, making 2025 and 2026 highly accessible years to visit. Carcassonne's airport continues to welcome low-cost flights from across Europe, and new train connections through the SNCF network make it easier than ever to reach the city from Paris, Toulouse, Bordeaux, or even Barcelona. Additionally, accommodations from historic boutique hotels within the Cité walls to charming countryside bed-and-breakfasts have been adapted with enhanced hospitality, flexible booking options, and thoughtful touches for today's travelers.

Sustainability is another reason these years are special. In response to growing environmental awareness, Carcassonne and the wider Occitanie region have committed to green tourism initiatives. Expect to find more options for eco-friendly stays, bike rentals, local farm-to-table restaurants, and guided walking tours that encourage low-impact exploration. Visiting during this time means supporting a city that is actively preserving its heritage while looking forward to a more conscious and balanced future.

From a visual standpoint, 2025 and 2026 will be breathtaking years to visit. In spring, blooming wildflowers line the canal banks and rolling hills beyond the Cité, while summer brings golden sunlight that enhances every photograph. Autumn transforms the vineyards into a vibrant palette of red and orange, offering some of the most scenic wine-tasting experiences in France. Even winter, often overlooked, bathes the city in a quiet, moody beauty that accentuates its medieval mystery.

Carcassonne is more than just a destination; it is a journey through time, a celebration of culture, and a retreat for the curious soul. Whether you are drawn by its history, charmed by its cuisine, or enticed by its architecture, the years 2025 and 2026 will give you the space, ambiance, and access to appreciate everything this remarkable place has to offer. It is a destination that continues to evolve while remaining rooted in the stories and stones of the past. In these upcoming years, Carcassonne is waiting not only to be seen but to be truly experienced.

CHAPTER 1

PLANNING YOUR TRIP

Best Times to Visit Carcassonne

Choosing the best time to visit Carcassonne can make a significant difference in your travel experience. Each season brings its own unique atmosphere, weather patterns, and rhythm of local life. Whether you're seeking sun-drenched days filled with festivals, peaceful walks along medieval walls, or a cozy winter retreat with fewer crowds, Carcassonne offers something rewarding in every part of the year. The key is knowing what to expect and aligning your travel preferences with the city's seasonal nuances.

Spring, from March to May, is one of the most pleasant times to explore Carcassonne. As winter fades, the weather becomes mild and inviting, with temperatures ranging from 12°C to 22°C. Nature begins to bloom in full color, painting the surrounding countryside with wildflowers and fresh greenery. The Canal du Midi sparkles in the spring light, and walking or biking along its tree-lined paths becomes a peaceful and scenic experience. Spring also sees the reawakening of local markets and outdoor terraces, where you can enjoy a coffee or meal under soft sunlight. With moderate tourist numbers and a host of cultural events beginning to appear on the calendar, spring is ideal for travelers who enjoy a relaxed atmosphere without missing out on local energy.

Summer, from June to August, is the most popular time to visit, and for good reason. The sun is almost guaranteed, with daytime temperatures often climbing to 30°C or more. This is festival season in Carcassonne, with the famous Festival de Carcassonne taking center stage in July. The entire city bursts into life with concerts, theater, dance, and open-air film screenings. The medieval Cité becomes especially animated, with costumed performers, live reenactments, and bustling night markets. However, with popularity comes crowds, particularly in July and August, when European holidaymakers descend upon the city. Prices for accommodations and tours are typically at their peak during this time. Still, if you thrive in lively atmospheres and want to experience Carcassonne in full swing, summer offers an unforgettable vibrancy.

Autumn, from September to November, is a favorite for many seasoned travelers. The intense heat of summer begins to mellow, creating ideal conditions for sightseeing and outdoor exploration. September in particular is still warm enough to enjoy alfresco dining and canal boat rides, while October and November bring a golden glow to the landscape as the region's vineyards prepare for harvest. Autumn is also a wonderful time to sample local wines and attend seasonal food festivals that highlight regional specialties like truffles, chestnuts, and game meats. The crowds begin to thin after September, making it easier to explore the Cité and surrounding areas at a leisurely pace. Lower accommodation rates and cooler temperatures make autumn a great blend of value, comfort, and culture.

Winter, from December to February, sees the fewest visitors, which may appeal to those seeking a more intimate and contemplative experience. Carcassonne takes on a quiet, almost mysterious charm in winter. Morning fog sometimes drapes over the fortress, creating an atmosphere that feels frozen in time. The Cité is still open to visitors, and without the usual crowds, you can enjoy the ramparts, basilica, and castle with more space and solitude. While some attractions may reduce hours or close temporarily for renovations, there's still much to enjoy. Local life continues at a slower pace, with cozy bistros serving cassoulet by the fire and Christmas markets bringing festive cheer to the Bastide Saint-Louis. Winter temperatures rarely fall below 3°C, and though snow is rare, it adds a magical touch when it does appear.

To summarize, the best time to visit Carcassonne depends on your personal travel style:

- If you enjoy warm weather and cultural events, summer offers the most dynamic experience, especially during the July festival season.
- If you prefer moderate temperatures, blooming landscapes, and fewer crowds, spring is an excellent choice.
- If you're after local flavor, stunning fall colors, and a calmer pace, autumn will reward you with rich experiences and better value.
- If you seek quiet beauty, introspective travel, and cozy atmospheres, winter may surprise you with its peaceful charm.

Regardless of when you choose to visit, Carcassonne's enduring beauty and historical significance remain constant. Its winding streets, towering ramparts, and sun-dappled squares await your discovery in every season. With thoughtful planning, your visit in 2025 or 2026 can align perfectly with your expectations and desires, ensuring that your time in this medieval jewel is as enriching as it is unforgettable.

How to Get to Carcassonne

Reaching Carcassonne is both straightforward and scenic, with several well-connected options for travelers coming from within France, across Europe, or even farther abroad. Whether you prefer flying directly into the region, taking the train through the picturesque French countryside, or driving at your own pace through vineyards and medieval villages, getting to Carcassonne is a journey that sets the tone for the rich experience that awaits.

For international travelers, the most convenient entry point is often via air. Carcassonne Airport, officially known as Aéroport de Carcassonne Salvaza, is a small but efficient airport located just about 4 kilometers from the city center. It offers regular flights from several major European cities, primarily through low-cost carriers. In particular, Ryanair operates seasonal and year-round flights connecting Carcassonne to destinations like London, Dublin, Brussels, and Porto. These flights make Carcassonne accessible for weekend breaks or longer stays without the need to connect through Paris or other major hubs. From the airport, reaching the city is quick and easy by taxi, shuttle, or rental car.

Another popular route is to fly into a larger international airport and continue to Carcassonne by train or car. Toulouse-Blagnac Airport, located approximately 100 kilometers to the west, is a major international airport with connections to North America, the Middle East, and various parts of Europe. From Toulouse, travelers can take a direct train to Carcassonne in just about an hour, or opt to drive and enjoy a scenic ride through the Occitanie region. Similarly, Montpellier-Méditerranée Airport to the east is another viable option, with train and road connections offering access to Carcassonne in under two hours.

Traveling by train is one of the most relaxing and environmentally friendly ways to arrive in Carcassonne. The city is served by the Gare de

Carcassonne, a central train station located in the lower town near the Canal du Midi. It is part of the SNCF national rail network and offers direct or connecting services from major French cities. From Paris, high-speed TGV and Intercités trains travel to Carcassonne in about 5 to 6 hours, usually with a connection in Toulouse or Narbonne. From Marseille or Lyon, the journey typically takes between 3 to 5 hours. The train ride itself is a highlight for many travelers, providing scenic views of rolling hills, sunflower fields, and medieval towns that capture the essence of southern France.

Driving to Carcassonne offers flexibility and the chance to explore the surrounding countryside at your leisure. The city is easily accessible via the A61 motorway, also known as the Autoroute des Deux Mers, which links Toulouse and Narbonne. Driving from Toulouse to Carcassonne takes roughly one hour, while from Montpellier it takes about two hours. Having a car can be especially beneficial if you plan to explore the vineyards, Cathar castles, or rural villages in the region. Parking is available both outside and inside the medieval Cité, though spaces inside the walls are limited and often restricted to hotel guests or permit holders. Most visitors prefer to park in designated lots nearby and walk into the historic core.

For those traveling within the Occitanie region, regional buses and carpooling services like BlaBlaCar also provide budget-friendly options. These services connect Carcassonne with nearby towns such as Narbonne, Béziers, and Albi. While buses may take longer than trains or cars, they can be an economical and flexible choice, particularly for short regional trips.

If you're arriving by bicycle or as part of a walking tour, Carcassonne is a rewarding destination along the Canal du Midi route. Cyclists can follow the canal's towpaths, which are part of a popular long-distance cycling route connecting Toulouse to the Mediterranean. This method of arrival is slower and requires some advance planning, but it offers an unmatched opportunity to approach Carcassonne in the most peaceful and picturesque manner.

No matter which method you choose, arriving in Carcassonne is an integral part of your travel story. The journey offers glimpses of the region's rich geography, rural charm, and ancient landscapes that set the scene for the adventure ahead. Whether you touch down at a nearby airport, roll in by train, or navigate the roads through vineyard-covered hills, your first sight of the Cité's towers rising in the distance will mark the beginning of a remarkable encounter with one of France's most magical cities.

Budgeting and Currency Tips

Planning your budget in advance can make your trip to Carcassonne smoother, more enjoyable, and free from unnecessary stress. Whether you're traveling on a tight budget or seeking a more luxurious experience, Carcassonne offers a wide range of options that can fit various travel styles. Understanding the local currency, payment habits, and general costs will help you make informed choices and enjoy your time without financial surprises.

Carcassonne, like the rest of France, uses the euro as its official currency. Bills come in denominations of 5, 10, 20, 50, 100, 200, and 500 euros, though it's rare to encounter the higher values in everyday transactions. Coins come in 1, 2, 5, 10, 20, and 50 cent pieces, as well as 1 and 2 euro coins. While credit and debit cards are widely accepted in hotels, restaurants, shops, and larger tourist attractions, it's always advisable to carry a small amount of cash, especially for purchases at open-air markets, small cafés, bakeries, and in more rural areas around Carcassonne where card readers might not always be available.

ATMs are plentiful in Carcassonne, particularly in the Bastide Saint-Louis and around the train station. Machines generally offer menus in multiple languages and accept major international cards. Be aware that your home bank may charge fees for international withdrawals, so check with them before you travel. To minimize costs, it's best to withdraw larger sums less frequently rather than making many small withdrawals. Most ATMs in France dispense 50-euro notes, so be sure to break these bills at larger establishments before trying to use them in small shops or buses, where change may be limited.

When it comes to budgeting your daily expenses, Carcassonne can be surprisingly affordable compared to bigger cities like Paris or Nice. For budget-conscious travelers, a daily spend of 50 to 70 euros per person is possible, covering hostel or budget hotel accommodation, public transportation, simple meals, and entry to select attractions. Mid-range travelers can expect to spend between 90 and 150 euros per day, which allows for a comfortable stay in a charming guesthouse or mid-tier hotel, a few meals out, guided tours, and more extensive sightseeing. Those looking for a luxury experience should plan for 200 euros or more per day, with upscale dining, boutique accommodations, and private experiences included.

Dining is an area where your budget can stretch or contract significantly. A meal at a local boulangerie or crêperie might cost as little as 5 to 10 euros, while a three-course dinner at a traditional French restaurant will generally range from 25 to 40 euros per person, excluding wine. Carcassonne is famous for its regional dish, cassoulet, which is hearty and filling—often enough to share—and can be found at a range of price points. Wine, often produced locally, is delicious and reasonably priced, with glasses available from around 3 to 5 euros in most restaurants.

Entrance to the medieval Cité is free to wander, but access to specific attractions such as the Château Comtal and the ramparts requires a ticket. Entry fees are modest, usually between 9 to 12 euros for adults, with discounts for children, students, and seniors. Many museums and cultural sites also offer free admission on the first Sunday of each month, especially in the off-season months, which can be a good way to explore on a budget.

Transportation within Carcassonne is another cost-effective aspect of your trip. The city is very walkable, particularly in the historic center, which reduces the need for taxis or rental cars. Local buses are available and inexpensive, with tickets costing around 1 euro per ride or a few euros for day passes. If you're planning to explore the region, car rentals are available but should be reserved in advance, especially during high season.

One important tip is to check whether your credit or debit card supports contactless payments and doesn't charge foreign transaction fees. Many establishments in France now accept contactless payments, making everyday purchases quick and convenient. It's also advisable to inform your bank of your travel plans to avoid any security holds on your card while abroad.

Tipping in France is not obligatory, as service is typically included in your restaurant bill. However, it is customary to leave small change or round up your bill as a gesture of appreciation. For example, if your bill is 18 euros, leaving 20 euros is a polite and well-received tip. For exceptional service or in more upscale establishments, a 5 to 10 percent tip is appreciated but not expected.

In terms of budgeting tools, consider using a travel expense tracking app or simply keeping a small travel journal to record your daily spend. This helps you stay on top of your budget and identify areas where you might want to splurge or cut back. Many travelers find that Carcassonne offers excellent value for money, particularly given the richness of its history, architecture, and culinary scene.

With a bit of planning and smart spending, your journey to Carcassonne in 2025 or 2026 can be both affordable and deeply enriching. Whether you're sipping local wine on a sunlit terrace or wandering the cobbled paths of the medieval fortress, you'll find that every euro spent goes a long way in creating an unforgettable experience in this extraordinary corner of southern France.

CHAPTER 2

GETTING AROUND CARCASSONNE

Walking the Medieval Streets

Walking is not only the most practical way to explore Carcassonne, it is by far the most rewarding. The city's layout, particularly within the historic Cité de Carcassonne, is designed for pedestrians, and its narrow cobbled lanes, stone archways, and winding alleyways are best experienced on foot. Unlike modern cities, where roads dominate the landscape, Carcassonne invites you to slow down, step back in time, and discover its many layers by wandering freely without a fixed agenda.

Inside the Cité, walking becomes more than just a mode of transport; it becomes a journey into the heart of medieval life. The entire walled fortress is pedestrianized, which allows visitors to explore in peace without the interruption of traffic or noise. You can follow the ancient paths once used by knights, merchants, and pilgrims, pausing to admire hidden courtyards, artisan shops, and architectural details that might otherwise go unnoticed. The uneven cobblestones and sloping alleys give the sensation of truly stepping back in time, immersing you in the atmosphere of a city that hasn't forgotten its past.

The Cité is compact but full of corners to explore. From the main entrance at the Narbonne Gate, your path may lead past souvenir stalls and cafés into quieter residential areas, shaded squares, and centuries-old chapels. Even during the busier summer months, it's possible to find peaceful nooks where you can sit, listen to the wind against the stone walls, and imagine the lives that once filled these streets. Early mornings and late evenings are particularly magical times to walk, as the golden light enhances the textures of the medieval architecture and the streets are empty of tourists.

Outside the Cité, the modern town of Carcassonne, particularly the Bastide Saint-Louis, is also ideal for walking. This area, located across the Aude River, is the heart of the lower town and follows a grid-like pattern laid out in the 13th century. Here, walking offers a different perspective less about history and more about local life. The Bastide is home to the central square, Place Carnot, where you can enjoy fresh produce markets, browse local shops, or relax at a street-side café and watch daily life unfold. The walk from the Cité to the Bastide takes roughly 15 to 20 minutes and includes the scenic Pont Vieux, an old stone bridge that offers sweeping views of the fortress and river below.

Walking between these two parts of the city offers a physical connection between Carcassonne's past and present. Along the way, you might pass by street performers, locals going about their day, or small exhibitions and festivals in open squares. During your stroll, keep an eye out for plaques and signs that provide historical context to the buildings and monuments around you; they often reveal surprising details that deepen your appreciation for the city.

Carcassonne also offers numerous walking trails beyond the city limits. From the Cité, there are marked walking paths leading to the banks of the Aude River and into the surrounding hills. These trails allow visitors to see the fortress from a distance, framed by natural scenery, and to discover hidden chapels, ancient ruins, and scenic viewpoints. A favorite among visitors is the Chemin de la Cavayère trail, which leads to a peaceful lake surrounded by woodland and picnic areas, making it ideal for a half-day escape from the city.

If you're interested in a more structured experience, guided walking tours are widely available and come in a variety of themes, from general history to the Cathar Crusade or culinary explorations. These tours typically last one to two hours and are led by knowledgeable locals who bring the city's history and legends to life through storytelling. Some are offered in the evening by lantern light, adding an extra layer of drama and enchantment to your experience.

A few practical tips will help make your walks through Carcassonne more enjoyable. First, wear comfortable shoes with good grip while the cobblestones are beautiful, they can be slippery, particularly after rain. Second, bring a reusable water bottle, especially in the summer months when the sun can be intense. Public water fountains are available in several locations. Lastly, while walking is safe and pleasant throughout the day, some areas within the Cité can become quite crowded in the middle of the day during high season. If you want a quieter experience, plan your walks in the early morning or later in the evening.

Carcassonne is a city made to be discovered step by step. Every walk reveals something new: a weathered doorway, a flower-filled balcony, or a breathtaking vista across the valley. There's no need to rush. Let your curiosity guide you and allow yourself to get lost in the maze of medieval streets. In Carcassonne, walking isn't just about getting from one place to another, it's about savoring the journey, feeling the layers of history beneath your feet, and letting the city unfold around you in its own time.

Public Transport and Bike Rentals

While Carcassonne is a highly walkable city, public transport and bike rentals offer convenient alternatives for getting around, especially when exploring areas beyond the central districts or planning excursions into the surrounding countryside. Whether you're traveling with family, managing heavy luggage, or simply prefer to conserve energy, the local transport options are affordable, accessible, and efficient for short- and mid-range travel within the city and nearby areas.

Carcassonne's public transportation system is managed by the RTCA (Régie des Transports de Carcassonne Agglo), which operates a network of bus routes throughout the city and its suburbs. Buses are a reliable way to move between the medieval Cité, the Bastide Saint-Louis, the train station, the airport, and residential districts. The bus system is especially useful for travelers staying in accommodations outside the central zones or for those planning to visit attractions that lie beyond walking distance, such as Lac de la Cavayère or outlying vineyards.

The city's buses are clean, punctual, and clearly marked, with schedules and route maps available at major stops, tourist information centers, and online. The main hub is located near Place Davilla in the lower town, making it easy to transfer between routes. Tickets can be purchased on board from the driver with cash, at ticket machines in some stations, or via the RTCA mobile app. A single ticket is typically valid for one hour of travel and costs around 1 euro, with options for day passes or multi-trip cards offering better value for those using the system regularly during their stay. Discounts are often available for students, seniors, and children.

Although Carcassonne is not a major urban center with a metro or tram network, the local buses run frequently during the day, especially during peak hours. Evening service is more limited, and most routes wind down after 8 or 9 PM. It's advisable to check timetables in advance if you plan to rely on buses for nighttime activities or early morning departures. Special shuttle services also connect the city center with Carcassonne Airport and Lac de la Cavayère during the summer, making them practical choices for arrivals and day trips.

In addition to buses, cycling is an increasingly popular and enjoyable way to get around Carcassonne, thanks to its compact size, relatively flat terrain in the lower town, and scenic routes along the Canal du Midi. Bike rentals are widely available from local shops in both the Bastide and near the Cité, with options ranging from classic city bikes to electric-assisted models for easier riding in hilly areas or on longer excursions. Prices typically start at 12 to 20 euros per day, with discounts for multi-day rentals and family packages. Helmets, locks, and child seats are often included or available for a small additional fee.

One of the most rewarding cycling routes in the area is the towpath along the Canal du Midi, a

UNESCO World Heritage Site that winds through the countryside with minimal car traffic. The shaded paths are perfect for leisurely rides past vineyards, small villages, and historic bridges. A popular route runs from Carcassonne to Trèbes, a charming town about 8 kilometers east, where you can stop for lunch by the canal and return at your own pace. For more ambitious cyclists, longer trails lead toward Narbonne or Castelnaudary, passing through a scenic mix of farmland and historic landscapes.

Cycling within the medieval Cité itself can be more challenging due to steep inclines, uneven cobblestones, and pedestrian-only zones. Most visitors choose to dismount and explore the fortress on foot, which is the best way to appreciate its narrow alleys and historic detail. However, cycling to and around the outer walls or using a bike to reach nearby viewpoints and picnic spots is both practical and enjoyable.

For eco-conscious travelers, combining walking, public buses, and bike rentals offers a sustainable and immersive way to explore the city. These methods reduce environmental impact, provide flexibility, and allow for spontaneous detours perhaps down a quiet residential lane or through a vineyard path that would otherwise be missed by car.

Overall, Carcassonne's manageable size and range of transport options mean that you can tailor your mobility to fit your travel style. Whether you hop on a bus to avoid midday heat, rent a bike for a countryside escape, or mix and match based on your plans, the infrastructure supports easy navigation without the need for a car. Public transport and bike rentals enhance your ability to move freely, access hidden corners, and engage with the city on your own terms one ride, one pedal, and one discovery at a time.

Accessibility and Navigation Tips

Navigating Carcassonne is generally straightforward due to its compact layout, clearly marked signs, and well-maintained streets. However, the city's medieval heritage, particularly within the walled Cité, can pose challenges for travelers with limited mobility, families with strollers, or anyone not accustomed to steep inclines and uneven surfaces. With the right preparation and a few local tips, getting around Carcassonne can be made easier and more enjoyable for travelers of all abilities.

The Cité de Carcassonne, while stunning, was built in an age when accessibility was not a priority.

Many of its narrow streets are paved with centuries-old cobblestones, and the elevation changes within the walls, especially around the Château Comtal and ramparts, can be difficult to navigate. Steps, sloped alleys, and uneven pathways are common, and handrails are often absent. Visitors who use wheelchairs or have mobility issues may find some sections of the Cité challenging or inaccessible altogether. That said, there are accessible routes into the Cité via the Narbonne Gate, and a limited number of shops, restaurants, and viewing areas are at ground level with no steps.

The good news is that the city of Carcassonne has made efforts in recent years to improve accessibility. Ramps have been added in several key areas of the Cité, and select public toilets are wheelchair-accessible. The visitor information center near the main entrance offers guidance on accessible routes and services, and some guided tours are adapted for visitors with special mobility needs. It is advisable to check with individual attractions in advance to confirm their accessibility status, as conditions can vary significantly from place to place.

In contrast, the Bastide Saint-Louis—the lower, more modern section of Carcassonne—is significantly easier to navigate. Its flat terrain, wide streets, and grid-like design make it suitable for all travelers, including those using wheelchairs, scooters, or strollers. Many of the city's services, shops, museums, and cafés are located in this area, and several accommodations offer rooms designed for accessibility. Public transportation, including the city's bus network, is generally equipped with low-floor buses and priority seating areas, and drivers are usually accommodating when assistance is needed.

When it comes to digital navigation, travelers will find that most online maps and navigation apps work well throughout Carcassonne. Google Maps, Apple Maps, and other location services offer detailed walking, driving, and public transport directions. Offline map apps, such as Maps.me or CityMaps2Go, are useful if you're planning to conserve data or if you're heading into the countryside where reception may be inconsistent. These tools can be especially helpful when exploring less-trafficked parts of the Bastide or finding your way back from canal-side walks and regional excursions.

Signage throughout Carcassonne is generally clear and well-placed. Directional signs pointing to key attractions such as the Château Comtal, Basilica of

Saints Nazarius and Celsus, and the Pont Vieux are found throughout the Cité. In the lower town, streets and public buildings are labeled, and walking routes are posted near major landmarks and intersections. Many signs include English translations, which help non-French speakers get around with minimal confusion.

For travelers driving into the city or renting a car for regional trips, it's important to note that vehicle access to the medieval Cité is highly restricted. Only residents, delivery vehicles, and guests of certain hotels within the walls are allowed to drive and park there. Most visitors are directed to park in designated lots outside the Cité, such as the large P1 and P2 parking zones. From there, it's a short uphill walk to the main gates. These parking areas are well-signposted and reasonably priced, with clear pedestrian paths leading into the fortress.

For added convenience, Carcassonne offers a seasonal tourist shuttle known as Le Petit Train or small electric buses that operate between the train station, Bastide Saint-Louis, and the Cité during peak months. These services are designed to ease the transition between major points of interest and reduce the strain of walking long distances in the summer heat. They are particularly helpful for visitors traveling with small children or those who may tire easily.

If you plan to explore the surrounding region, GPS systems work reliably throughout the Occitanie countryside. Whether you're driving to a Cathar castle, navigating a bike route along the Canal du Midi, or walking to a nearby vineyard, using a combination of digital and traditional navigation methods is recommended. Carrying a printed map or regional brochure from the tourist office can be useful in more rural areas where signage might be sparse or only in French.

Overall, the key to navigating Carcassonne successfully lies in balancing spontaneity with a bit of planning. While the medieval charm of the Cité may limit full accessibility in some parts, the city's friendly locals, modern amenities, and thoughtful infrastructure make it possible for most travelers to enjoy a fulfilling visit. Whether you're strolling the boulevards of the Bastide or climbing to a panoramic viewpoint on the ramparts, Carcassonne invites you to move at your own pace, explore with curiosity, and embrace the layered textures of a city shaped by history and still alive with possibility.

CHAPTER 3

WHERE TO STAY

Best Areas for First-Time Visitors

Choosing where to stay in Carcassonne is one of the most important decisions you'll make when planning your trip. The city offers a variety of neighborhoods and accommodation styles, each with its own distinct character and advantages. For first-time visitors, selecting the right area will not only enhance your comfort but also influence how you experience the city from how much walking or transportation you'll need, to how close you are to major attractions, dining, and shopping. Whether you're drawn to medieval charm, local life, or riverside tranquility, Carcassonne has a perfect corner waiting for you.

The most iconic and atmospheric place to stay is inside the Cité de Carcassonne, the walled medieval fortress that draws travelers from around the world. This UNESCO World Heritage Site offers a fairy-tale experience, especially at night when the day-trippers leave and the fortress becomes quiet and dreamlike. Within the Cité's ramparts, you'll find a limited but enchanting selection of boutique hotels, charming guesthouses, and romantic inns, some of which are set in buildings that date back centuries. Staying here allows you to wander the cobbled lanes before breakfast, enjoy sunset views over the walls, and explore the castle and basilica in relative solitude outside peak hours. However, accommodations here tend to be more expensive and can book up months in advance, especially in high season. Also, because the streets are mostly car-free and uneven, guests with mobility concerns or lots of luggage may find it a bit challenging.

Just across the Aude River from the Cité lies the Trivalle district, a picturesque and quieter area that offers stunning views of the fortress and easy walking access via the Pont Vieux, the city's old bridge. Trivalle is ideal for those who want to be close to the medieval action without actually staying inside the fortress walls. This neighborhood is filled with small hotels, B&Bs, local restaurants, and cafés with outdoor seating. Its location makes it a natural base for walking tours, photography, and relaxing riverside strolls. The ambiance here is more laid-back, with fewer crowds and a more residential feel than the Cité itself.

For a more modern and practical experience, the Bastide Saint-Louis, or the "Lower Town," is an excellent choice. Located on the opposite side of the Aude River from the Cité, the Bastide is Carcassonne's commercial and administrative center, originally built in the 13th century as a planned town. This area offers a wider range of accommodations at varying price points, from budget-friendly hotels to contemporary apartments. The grid-like layout makes it easy to navigate, and the area is home to many restaurants, shops, museums, and markets. Place Carnot, the main square, is a lively hub for dining and people-watching. Staying in the Bastide gives you a taste of local life and places you closer to train and bus connections, making it especially convenient for first-time visitors using public transportation.

Another appealing option for travelers looking for a peaceful, natural setting is the area around Canal du Midi. A bit further from the central action, this area is perfect for those who appreciate quiet surroundings and scenic beauty. Accommodations here range from canal-side guesthouses to countryside lodges and boutique retreats. The canal's tree-lined paths are ideal for walking and cycling, and some properties offer direct access to boat tours or nature trails. It's a great choice for couples, older travelers, or anyone seeking a slower, more restful pace while still being a short taxi or bus ride from the Cité and the Bastide.

For travelers with a car, the outskirts of Carcassonne provide several attractive possibilities. Staying slightly outside the city gives you access to larger hotel chains, agritourism-style bed and breakfasts, and even vineyard stays in the surrounding countryside. These rural locations offer great value, beautiful views, and a chance to explore beyond the city, including Cathar castles, local wineries, and peaceful villages. If you plan to visit nearby sites like Montolieu, Limoux, or the Cabardès wine region, this can be a strategic and rewarding choice. Do note that having a car is almost essential in these areas, as public transport options are limited.

When deciding where to stay, think carefully about your travel goals. If your priority is immersing yourself in medieval history and atmosphere, the

Cité or Trivalle are unmatched. If convenience, transportation, and everyday amenities are more important, the Bastide Saint-Louis may be your best fit. For tranquility and nature, the Canal du Midi area and the surrounding countryside offer unforgettable charm. Each neighborhood tells a different side of Carcassonne's story, and for first-time visitors, the right choice can transform a good trip into a truly exceptional one.

No matter where you choose to stay, Carcassonne's manageable size means that you're never too far from its key attractions. With thoughtful planning, you'll be well positioned to explore the city's medieval wonders, taste its regional flavors, and relax in accommodations that match your pace, style, and curiosity.

Boutique Hotels and Charming Guesthouses

Carcassonne is a city where history and hospitality blend seamlessly, and nowhere is that more evident than in its selection of boutique hotels and charming guesthouses. For travelers seeking a stay that goes beyond the ordinary, these accommodations offer a more intimate, personalized, and memorable experience than standard hotel chains. Often family-run, and frequently located in historic buildings, boutique hotels and guesthouses in Carcassonne reflect the spirit of the city, elegant, welcoming, and rich with stories.

Inside the medieval Cité, boutique hotels are housed in centuries-old structures that have been carefully restored and adapted to modern comfort while preserving their architectural integrity. Stone walls, exposed beams, antique furnishings, and flower-filled courtyards are common features. The number of rooms is usually small ranging from five to twenty which adds to the sense of exclusivity and quiet. Some properties even offer direct views of the ramparts or the castle, making it possible to fall asleep while gazing at the softly lit towers of the fortress. The peaceful atmosphere after dark, when the crowds have thinned and the old city seems to sigh with ancient stories, is a particular highlight for those staying within the walls.

One of the advantages of boutique hotels in Carcassonne is the level of personal service. Unlike large hotels, where interactions can feel impersonal, many of these establishments are run by owners who live on-site and take pride in offering warm, attentive care to their guests. They are often happy to share insider tips about the best local restaurants, less-visited sights, and upcoming cultural events. Breakfasts are typically served in a cozy dining room or courtyard and may feature homemade jams, fresh pastries, and regional specialties like local cheeses or cassoulet.

Charming guesthouses, also known as chambres d'hôtes in French, offer a homestay-like experience with a focus on authenticity and connection. These are especially popular in the neighborhoods just outside the Cité, such as Trivalle and the areas along the Aude River. Here, you might stay in a converted 18th-century townhouse, a vine-covered cottage, or a country-style villa with a garden. Rooms are individually decorated, often reflecting the owner's personal taste and love for the region. Some guesthouses include access to outdoor terraces, private pools, or even small libraries filled with books on local history and culture.

One of the most delightful aspects of staying in a guesthouse is the opportunity to meet other travelers in a communal, home-like setting. Shared breakfasts or evening aperitifs provide moments for casual conversation, cultural exchange, and often the sharing of travel tips. Hosts frequently go the extra mile organizing wine tastings, helping with restaurant reservations, or offering pick-up from the train station. It's this combination of comfort and connection that makes guesthouses a favorite for solo travelers, couples, and small groups alike.

In the Bastide Saint-Louis, you'll find a selection of boutique accommodations that combine old-world charm with urban convenience. These properties offer easy access to restaurants, museums, shops, and public transport, making them a great option for travelers who want to balance historical exploration with modern amenities. Many of the buildings in this area date back to the 17th and 18th centuries and feature high ceilings, wrought iron balconies, and large windows that flood the rooms with light. Interiors are often stylishly updated with a mix of antique décor and contemporary comfort, creating a space that feels both classic and fresh.

Whether you choose a boutique hotel nestled within the medieval Cité or a welcoming guesthouse near the river, you'll benefit from the kind of charm and personality that only independent, small-scale lodging can offer. These accommodations not only provide a comfortable base for your explorations, they become a meaningful part of your overall experience. You'll remember the lavender in the garden, the clink of breakfast cups in a sunlit courtyard, or the host who pointed you to a hidden viewpoint at sunset.

For travelers in 2025 and 2026, advance booking is recommended, particularly during spring and summer when demand peaks. These places often have loyal returning guests and limited availability, so early reservations will give you more options and better prices. Be sure to read reviews carefully to find a property that aligns with your preferences for location, atmosphere, and level of service.

In Carcassonne, where the past is ever-present and the pace of life invites you to slow down and savor every detail, boutique hotels and charming guesthouses offer more than just a place to sleep; they offer a chance to live, however briefly, in a storybook setting. Whether tucked away on a quiet medieval street or opening onto a leafy courtyard near the river, these stays are sure to become one of the most treasured parts of your journey.

Family-Friendly and Budget Accommodations

Carcassonne, with its fairy-tale fortress, lively town squares, and accessible size, is a fantastic destination for families and travelers on a budget. While it's easy to be enchanted by the romantic charm of boutique hotels, the city also offers a wide variety of practical, welcoming, and affordable lodging options that cater to families, groups, students, and anyone looking to stretch their travel funds without sacrificing comfort or convenience.

From budget hotels and youth hostels to family-run guesthouses and self-catering apartments, Carcassonne proves that you don't need to spend a fortune to enjoy an unforgettable stay.

For families, staying in a location that offers space, safety, and access to kid-friendly activities is essential. The Bastide Saint-Louis in the lower town is one of the best areas for family travelers. It offers relatively flat streets that are easy to navigate with strollers or young children, and it's close to playgrounds, markets, and public transport. Several mid-range and budget hotels in this district offer family rooms or adjoining rooms that allow parents and children to stay comfortably together. Many of these establishments include breakfast and provide extra beds or cribs upon request.

Self-catering apartments and holiday rentals are especially popular among families. These accommodations offer the space and flexibility to cook meals, do laundry, and settle into a routine, which can be a great relief on longer trips. Many apartments in Carcassonne come fully equipped with kitchens, dining areas, and washing machines, making them perfect for families with young kids or travelers on extended stays. Options range from modern studios in the Bastide to historic apartments with views of the Cité, often available through platforms like Airbnb or local rental agencies. Booking early is key, especially during summer and school holiday periods.

Carcassonne also offers a number of budget hotels and motels, many of which are part of reliable national chains like Ibis Budget, B&B Hotels, or Première Classe. These hotels are generally located just outside the city center or along main access roads, providing basic but clean and efficient lodging. They are ideal for travelers arriving by car or looking for a simple place to sleep after a long day of sightseeing. While amenities are minimal, these hotels often offer 24-hour check-in, parking, and buffet breakfasts at very affordable rates. For budget-conscious visitors, they represent excellent value and convenience.

Another great option for low-cost lodging is the city's youth hostel, the Auberge de Jeunesse Carcassonne, located just outside the medieval Cité. This hostel offers dormitory beds and private rooms at very reasonable prices, along with shared kitchen facilities, lockers, and common areas where travelers can meet and relax. It is especially popular with solo travelers, backpackers, and students. The hostel's location is a major perk within walking distance of the Cité and the Bastide making it a strategic base for sightseeing without needing transportation.

For travelers with a car, camping grounds and caravan parks around Carcassonne offer an alternative that combines budget-friendly accommodation with a connection to nature. Several sites near the Canal du Midi or Lac de la Cavayère provide tent pitches, mobile home rentals, and family-friendly amenities like pools, playgrounds, and bike rentals. These are excellent options during the warmer months and are often favored by European families on summer road trips. The relaxed atmosphere and outdoor setting make them ideal for those who want a slower pace and room for children to play.

When booking budget accommodation in Carcassonne, it's important to consider a few factors beyond just the nightly rate. Check for added fees, such as city taxes or cleaning charges, which may not be included in the advertised price. Review policies on late check-ins, breakfast options, and whether the location is well connected to public transport if you're not driving. Booking directly with the property can sometimes result in better rates or flexible cancellation policies compared to third-party platforms.

Despite being more affordable, many budget and family-friendly accommodations still offer charming touches like local décor, helpful hosts, and personal recommendations for exploring the city. Staff at smaller family-run hotels and guesthouses are often eager to assist with restaurant reservations, maps, and tips on attractions suitable for kids or free events happening in town.

In the end, staying in Carcassonne on a budget doesn't mean missing out on its magic. Whether you're watching the sunset over the fortress from a riverside apartment, enjoying a picnic in a leafy campground, or sharing stories with fellow travelers in a hostel lounge, you'll find that the warmth of the city extends well beyond its ancient stones. With so many options that blend affordability, comfort, and convenience, Carcassonne welcomes all travelers, families, backpackers, and bargain-seekers alike to experience its medieval wonders without breaking the bank.

CHAPTER 4

WHAT TO EAT AND DRINK

<u>Traditional Languedoc Cuisine</u>

Carcassonne is not only a destination for lovers of history and architecture it is also a treasure trove for food enthusiasts eager to explore the rich, hearty flavors of southern France. As the capital of the Aude department and one of the key cities in the Languedoc region, Carcassonne serves as an ideal gateway to the culinary traditions of Occitanie, a land known for its rustic dishes, local wines, and Mediterranean influences. Here, meals are more than nourishment; they are an expression of the region's soul, shaped by centuries of peasant wisdom, noble feasts, and seasonal rhythms.

At the heart of Carcassonne's culinary identity is cassoulet, the region's most iconic dish. This slow-cooked white bean stew, traditionally prepared with duck confit, pork sausages, and pieces of goose or pork belly, is more than a meal; it's a symbol of the land's agricultural roots and deeply ingrained traditions. Served bubbling hot in an earthenware dish, cassoulet is a hearty and filling dish that's best enjoyed at a leisurely pace with a glass of local red wine. Each town in the region lays claim to its own variation Castelnaudary, Toulouse, and Carcassonne all defend their cassoulet as the most authentic. Carcassonne's version often includes partridge or other game meats when available, giving it a distinctive local twist.

The cuisine of Languedoc is shaped by the region's natural abundance of sun-drenched vineyards, olive groves, fields of lentils and wheat, and the bounty of the Mediterranean. Duck is a frequent star of the table, appearing not just in cassoulet but also in magret de canard (duck breast) and confit de canard (duck leg preserved in its own fat), both of which are flavorful and tender when prepared in the traditional style. Lamb and pork, often slow-roasted or braised with garlic and herbs, are also common, and many dishes are enriched with local olive oil and aromatic herbs like thyme, rosemary, and bay leaf.

Seafood plays a lesser but still important role, especially in dishes that reflect the broader Occitanie region's connection to the Mediterranean. Mussels, anchovies, and salted cod are incorporated into regional recipes such as brandade de morue, a creamy salt cod purée often flavored with garlic and olive oil. You'll also find dishes like bourride, a kind of fish stew, and seafood platters served in restaurants that source from nearby coastal towns.

Vegetables are celebrated in their seasonal forms and often appear in dishes like ratatouille, tian (a Provençal-style vegetable bake), and simple roasted or stewed preparations. Lentils from the Languedoc highlands, white haricot beans, and earthy mushrooms from the Montagne Noire are all staples that make their way into local recipes. Even side dishes, such as aligot (a cheesy mashed potato dish with garlic and tomme cheese), offer comforting flavors and textures that highlight the region's rustic charm.

Cheese lovers will be delighted with the variety of artisanal cheeses available in and around Carcassonne. Goat's cheese is especially popular, ranging from fresh and creamy to aged and tangy. Pélardon, a soft goat cheese from the Cévennes, is a local favorite, often drizzled with honey or served warm over salad. Cow's milk cheeses like Tomme de Pyrénées and blue-veined Roquefort from nearby regions are also readily available, particularly in local markets and cheese shops.

Of course, no exploration of traditional Languedoc cuisine would be complete without discussing the local wines. Carcassonne sits in the heart of one of France's largest wine-producing regions, and its surrounding hills are blanketed with vineyards that produce bold reds, crisp whites, and refreshing rosés. The wines of the Minervois and Corbières appellations are particularly prominent. These wines are robust and earthy, often made from Grenache, Syrah, Mourvèdre, and Carignan grapes. They pair beautifully with the rich, meaty dishes of the region. Sparkling wine lovers should not miss Blanquette de Limoux, one of the world's oldest sparkling wines, produced just a short drive from Carcassonne and predating even Champagne.

Traditional desserts in Carcassonne and the Languedoc region reflect a love of simple, sweet pleasures. You'll find fougasse sucrée, a sweetened bread with sugar and sometimes orange blossom water, and croustade aux pommes, a flaky apple tart often made with layers of thin dough brushed with butter. Dried fruits, almonds, and honey also appear in many sweets, revealing the region's ties to both Mediterranean and mountain traditions.

Dining in Carcassonne is not about rushing through a meal. It's about enjoying the process—savoring each bite, sharing dishes with friends or family, and engaging in lively conversation in a cozy bistro or on a terrace overlooking the medieval walls. Restaurants range from family-owned taverns serving time-honored recipes to upscale establishments reinterpreting local classics with modern flair. Weekly markets provide opportunities to sample cheeses, charcuterie, baked goods, and seasonal produce directly from farmers and artisans, bringing the spirit of the region into your own hands.

Whether you're indulging in a rich cassoulet on a chilly evening, sipping a chilled rosé on a summer patio, or sampling local cheeses under the vaulted ceiling of a centuries-old inn, traditional Languedoc cuisine is central to your experience of Carcassonne. It tells the story of the land, the people, and the culture in every course and invites you to become part of that story, one delicious meal at a time.

Best Restaurants, Cafés, and Markets

Carcassonne's culinary scene is a vibrant mix of rustic tradition, regional pride, and contemporary flair. Whether you're seeking a candlelit dinner in a medieval inn, a relaxed lunch on a sun-drenched terrace, or the lively buzz of a local market, the city offers abundant opportunities to savor the flavors of Languedoc and beyond. From hidden cafés tucked into cobbled alleyways to open-air market stalls brimming with fresh produce and local specialties, Carcassonne is a place where food isn't just a necessity, it's a celebration of life.

Inside the walled Cité, many of the most atmospheric restaurants are found nestled among stone ramparts and medieval towers. These establishments range from upscale dining rooms to cozy bistros with wooden beams and flickering candles. One of the most renowned is La Barbacane, located in the luxurious Hôtel de la Cité. This Michelin-starred restaurant offers a refined take on traditional Languedoc cuisine, with exquisite presentations, fine local wines, and an ambience that's both romantic and regal. For those celebrating a special occasion, La Barbacane delivers an unforgettable dining experience.

For something more casual yet equally satisfying, Restaurant Comte Roger, also within the Cité, offers a beautifully shaded terrace and a reputation for one of the best cassoulets in town. Their menu blends regional staples like duck confit and foie gras with seasonal vegetables and inventive touches. Reservations are recommended, especially during high season, as the restaurant is a favorite among both locals and travelers.

If you're looking for a relaxed spot for lunch or a light dinner, Le Jardin de la Tour is a charming option hidden behind the Cité's main thoroughfare. With its flower-filled courtyard and rustic décor, it provides a peaceful respite from the crowds. Their menu features fresh, regional ingredients and changes with the seasons. You'll find hearty salads, grilled meats, and flavorful vegetarian options, making it a versatile choice for various palates.

Crossing over the Pont Vieux into the Bastide Saint-Louis opens up a wider range of dining experiences. The lower town is home to many excellent restaurants offering good value and authentic cuisine. Le Bistro d'Augustin, near the train station, is a favorite for traditional French fare served in a warm, welcoming environment. Here you can try regional classics like duck breast with honey, roasted vegetables, and house-made desserts at reasonable prices.

Another standout is L'Escargot, located near Place Carnot. This bistro-style eatery focuses on tapas and small plates with a French twist, encouraging guests to sample and share a variety of dishes. It's particularly popular in the evening when locals gather to enjoy aperitifs and bite-sized specialties. For a true local experience, consider arriving early and settling in for a leisurely meal that stretches into the night.

When it comes to cafés, Carcassonne is rich with options that are ideal for a mid-morning coffee, an afternoon pastry, or a simple glass of wine as the sun sets. Café Saillan on Place Carnot is a long-standing favorite with locals, offering strong espresso, fresh croissants, and excellent people-watching in the heart of the Bastide. Another gem is Chez Félix, a small café that exudes charm and serves fresh tarts, quiches, and regional wines in a cozy setting just a few steps from the river. Many of these cafés also offer prix-fixe lunch menus during the week, which are a great value and a wonderful way to experience home-style cooking.

No culinary exploration of Carcassonne would be complete without a visit to the local markets, which remain a central part of life in the region. The Place Carnot market, held every Tuesday, Thursday, and Saturday morning, is the most vibrant. On these days, the square fills with stalls selling everything from seasonal fruits and vegetables to cheeses, olives, cured meats, and freshly baked breads. You'll also find regional specialties like tapenade, honey from the Montagne Noire, and local wines and liqueurs. The market is a feast for the senses, bright colors, enticing aromas, and the animated chatter of vendors and customers filling the air.

For those looking to prepare their own meals or pack a picnic, this market is an essential stop. It's also a perfect place to interact with local producers and learn more about the region's agricultural heritage. Many vendors are happy to offer samples, and even a brief exchange in French is usually met with a smile. For visitors staying in self-catering apartments or countryside gîtes, the market provides an ideal way to stock up on fresh, local ingredients.

In addition to Place Carnot, smaller neighborhood markets and specialty food shops, boulangeries, fromageries, and charcuteries dot the city, particularly in the Bastide. These shops are perfect for grabbing a quick bite, assembling a cheese board, or purchasing edible souvenirs to take home. Many shops proudly display their local origins, labeling products from nearby villages and family farms, which ensures that you're tasting the true flavors of Occitanie.

Carcassonne's culinary scene may be rooted in tradition, but it is far from stagnant. New chefs and restaurateurs are continually bringing fresh ideas and influences to the table, creating a dynamic food culture that respects the past while embracing the future. Whether you're dining beneath a vaulted ceiling in the Cité, sipping coffee on a bustling square, or wandering a market under the southern sun, the city offers endless ways to eat well and eat local.

In the end, what makes dining in Carcassonne so special is the sense of place that infuses every bite and every meal. The ingredients, the recipes, the settings all reflect the history, pride, and generosity of the region. It's not just about food; it's about connection to the land, to the culture, and to the moment you're in.

Local Wines and Regional Specialties

Carcassonne sits in the heart of one of the most prolific and storied wine-producing regions in France. Surrounded by rolling vineyards and centuries-old estates, the city offers travelers a golden opportunity to taste the very soul of the Languedoc region through its wines, its time-honored culinary specialties, and its devotion to locally grown, seasonal ingredients. Whether you are sipping a bold red under the shade of a plane tree, sampling a crisp white in a riverside bistro, or indulging in the area's rich, meaty dishes, every experience reveals a deeper layer of Carcassonne's character.

The most celebrated wines around Carcassonne come from the Corbières and Minervois appellations, both of which lie just a short drive from the city. These AOCs (Appellations d'Origine Contrôlée) produce red, white, and rosé wines, but they are best known for their robust reds made from grape varieties like Grenache, Syrah, Mourvèdre, and Carignan. The terrain—sun-baked hills, rocky soils, and windswept valleys—gives the wines a distinct minerality and intensity, often accompanied by flavors of dark berries, dried herbs, and a touch of spice. These reds pair beautifully with the hearty dishes of the region, especially cassoulet, grilled lamb, and duck confit.

Minervois wines, produced north of the Aude River, tend to be smooth and well-structured, with a pleasing balance between fruitiness and earthiness. They are excellent companions to both red meats and aged cheeses. Corbières wines, meanwhile, are known for their complexity and deep character, often described as "wild" or "untamed" due to the rugged landscape in which they are produced. Visiting a vineyard or wine cave in either appellation is highly recommended. Many offer tours, tastings, and the opportunity to learn about the ancient winegrowing traditions that have shaped the culture here.

Beyond these well-known appellations, Carcassonne is also a gateway to one of France's most unique sparkling wines: Blanquette de Limoux. Produced just 30 kilometers south of the city, this sparkling wine is believed to be the oldest of its kind in the world, predating Champagne by more than a century. Made primarily from the Mauzac grape, along with Chardonnay and Chenin Blanc, Blanquette de Limoux is fresh, elegant, and slightly floral, with gentle bubbles and a refined finish. It's an ideal apéritif or a festive choice for celebrations and romantic dinners.

Another notable variant is Crémant de Limoux, also produced in the Limoux area using the méthode traditionnelle. While similar to Champagne in process, Crémant de Limoux often has a more delicate and fruit-forward profile, making it an appealing and often more affordable alternative. Wine lovers should take the time to visit a cellar in Limoux or pick up a bottle at Carcassonne's markets and specialty shops to enjoy a sparkling taste of the region's history.

To accompany these wines, Carcassonne offers a wide range of regional specialties that reflect the flavors of the land and the legacy of rural cooking. One of the most iconic is cassoulet, a slow-cooked stew of white beans, duck confit, pork sausage, and sometimes game meats. Rich and deeply flavorful, cassoulet is the perfect dish to enjoy with a full-bodied Minervois or Corbières red. Though many restaurants serve cassoulet year-round, it's especially satisfying in the cooler months when its warmth and heartiness are most appreciated.

Another local favorite is aligot, a creamy blend of mashed potatoes, cheese (typically tomme or cantal), and garlic, stirred until elastic and silky. While originally from the neighboring region of Aubrac, aligot has found a home on the menus of rustic Carcassonne eateries. It is often served as a side to grilled meats or sausages.

Charcuterie is another standout category in the regional culinary scene. Duck pâté, foie gras, country-style terrines, and cured hams are widely available in both restaurants and markets. Often served with crusty bread, pickled vegetables, and a glass of red wine, these items offer a simple yet luxurious dining experience. Foie gras, in particular, is a specialty in the region and is frequently served with a touch of fig jam or onion confit to balance its richness.

Cheese lovers will also find plenty to savor in and around Carcassonne. Goat's cheeses are especially common, ranging from fresh and soft to aged and firm. Pélardon, a small round goat cheese from the Cévennes, is often sold in markets and frequently appears on cheese boards in local restaurants. Sheep's milk cheeses and mountain varieties like tomme de Pyrénées are also popular and pair beautifully with local red and white wines.

For something sweet, regional desserts offer a delightful end to any meal. Croustade aux pommes, a flaky apple pastry often made with layers of stretched dough, is a specialty of the area. Some versions include a splash of Armagnac or a touch of citrus zest to enhance the flavor. Almonds, honey, and dried fruits are also common in local sweets, reflecting the Mediterranean influence on the region's cuisine.

To fully immerse yourself in the tastes of Carcassonne, a visit to one of the city's artisan food shops or weekly markets is essential. Here, you can sample local olive oils, artisan vinegars, herbes de

Provence, tapenade, and handcrafted confections. Many vendors will offer samples, allowing you to taste before you buy and discover new favorites.

Whether you're enjoying a leisurely meal in a stone-walled tavern, sipping a local wine on a shaded patio, or browsing a market stall filled with seasonal delights, the food and drink of Carcassonne will linger in your memory long after your visit ends. These regional specialties and wines are more than culinary traditions; they are expressions of the land's history, the resilience of its people, and the joy of simple, honest pleasures shared around a table.

CHAPTER 5

CULTURE AND TRADITIONS

Festivals and Annual Events

Carcassonne may be best known for its majestic medieval walls and fairytale appearance, but the city is far from frozen in time. Throughout the year, it comes alive with a diverse calendar of festivals and cultural events that celebrate its rich heritage, vibrant local life, and deep connection to the arts. These festivals offer an immersive window into the traditions of southern France, blending music, food, history, theater, and fireworks in ways that draw both locals and travelers into the spirit of celebration. Whether you're visiting in spring, summer, autumn, or winter, chances are you'll find yourself swept up in one of Carcassonne's signature events.

The crown jewel of the city's festival calendar is the Festival de Carcassonne, held annually throughout the month of July. This month-long cultural extravaganza is one of the most important performing arts festivals in France, transforming both the medieval Cité and the Bastide into grand stages for music, theater, dance, and opera. Internationally renowned artists and local performers alike take to open-air stages, castle courtyards, and historic squares. The lineup spans classical concerts, jazz ensembles, contemporary pop and rock performances, and traditional French chansons. Many of the performances take place at the Théâtre Jean-Deschamps, an open-air amphitheater nestled within the ramparts of the Cité, where the combination of world-class music and ancient architecture creates an unforgettable experience.

Just as iconic is Bastille Day on July 14th, when Carcassonne hosts one of the most spectacular fireworks displays in France. Known as the "Feu d'Artifice de la Cité," this pyrotechnic show lights up the sky above the fortress in a dazzling cascade of color, music, and light. Tens of thousands of spectators gather on both sides of the Aude River to witness the visual spectacle, which pays homage to French unity and independence. Viewing spots fill up early in the day, so bringing a picnic and staking out a place along the riverbanks or on the Pont Vieux can be part of the experience. For many, this event alone is reason enough to plan a visit to Carcassonne in mid-July.

In spring and early summer, Carcassonne becomes a hub of local celebration with events like the Fête de la Musique on June 21st. Held throughout France, this day-long music festival brings amateur and professional musicians into the streets, performing everything from classical quartets to electronic beats. In Carcassonne, the event spills into every corner from quiet courtyards and bustling squares to riverside cafés and the medieval streets of the Cité. It's a joyous, open celebration of music and community, and best of all, it's free to attend.

Autumn brings a more relaxed but no less engaging atmosphere with the Salon du Livre, Carcassonne's annual book fair. Held in the Bastide, the fair features author talks, book signings, workshops, and exhibitions. It draws writers and readers from across the Occitanie region and offers a great opportunity to engage with French literature and publishing. For those with an interest in language, storytelling, or

French culture, it provides a quieter but enriching alternative to the high-energy events of summer.

Winter also has its own charms. December sees the city dressed in holiday lights for Marché de Noël, the Christmas market held in Place Carnot and around the Bastide. Wooden chalets offer regional crafts, seasonal treats, mulled wine, and handmade gifts, while an ice-skating rink and carousel delight younger visitors. Though less internationally known, this market captures the warmth and coziness of French holiday traditions and is a wonderful way to experience Carcassonne in a quieter, more intimate setting.

In addition to these major events, smaller festivals and celebrations are held throughout the year. The Festival de Magie in February showcases magic and illusion with performances for both adults and children. In May, the Fête du Vin honors local winemakers with tastings, vineyard tours, and festive gatherings in and around the city. Various food fairs, open-air theater events, and historical reenactments also occur throughout the year, particularly in spring and early fall.

Many of Carcassonne's festivals highlight its deep connection to history, and some events include reenactments of medieval jousts, parades in period costumes, and storytelling sessions centered on Cathar legends. These experiences, while often family-friendly and entertaining, also deepen visitors' understanding of the city's layered past and cultural identity.

For travelers planning a visit, it's a good idea to check the city's tourism website or local event listings in advance to align your itinerary with upcoming festivals. Many events are free or reasonably priced, and most are walkable from central accommodations. Participation in these gatherings not only enhances your trip with joyful memories but also supports local artists, artisans, and traditions.

Carcassonne's festivals and annual events bring the city to life in ways that no guidebook or tour can fully capture. They offer a rare opportunity to see the city not just as a historic monument, but as a living, breathing community that celebrates its heritage while embracing the energy of today. Whether it's the thunderous applause at a summer concert within ancient walls or the quiet joy of sipping hot chocolate at the Christmas market, these moments form the heartbeat of a truly immersive Carcassonne experience.

Language, Customs, and Etiquette

Understanding the language, customs, and etiquette of Carcassonne and more broadly, the Occitanie region can greatly enhance your travel experience. While Carcassonne is a popular destination that welcomes thousands of international visitors each year, it remains proudly rooted in its regional identity and cultural traditions. Taking the time to appreciate these subtleties will not only help you navigate the city more easily but also create deeper, more meaningful connections with locals and the places you visit.

French is the official language of Carcassonne, and while English is widely understood in hotels, tourist attractions, and some restaurants, especially during peak tourist seasons, it is not universally spoken. Outside of the most touristic areas, you may find that shopkeepers, market vendors, or local residents speak little or no English. This is not a sign of unfriendliness, but rather a reflection of the region's strong French and Occitan roots. Making an effort to learn a few key phrases in French is appreciated and can make your interactions smoother and more enjoyable. Simple greetings like "bonjour" (good day), "s'il vous plaît" (please), "merci" (thank you), and "au revoir" (goodbye) go a long way. Attempting to start a conversation in French even if just a few words shows respect and effort, and you'll often be met with kindness and patience in return.

Carcassonne is located in the Occitanie region, a part of France with its own cultural history, including the ancient Occitan language. While Occitan is not widely spoken today, it still influences local place names, folklore, music, and even cuisine. You may see bilingual signs in French and Occitan, and some local festivals or events may feature traditional Occitan songs and dances. These cultural expressions are cherished by the community and offer a glimpse into the distinct identity of the region beyond mainstream French culture.

As in most parts of France, social etiquette in Carcassonne places a strong emphasis on politeness and respect. When entering a shop, café, or restaurant, it is customary to greet the staff with "bonjour" or "bonsoir" (good evening), depending on the time of day. Failing to greet someone before asking a question or making a purchase can be perceived as rude. Similarly, saying "merci" when receiving service or assistance is expected and appreciated. If you're in a more formal setting, adding "madame" or "monsieur" to your greeting shows additional courtesy.

Mealtimes are considered important moments of the day, often enjoyed slowly and without rush. It is customary to wait to be seated in most restaurants, even in casual ones. Tipping is not obligatory in France, as service is included in the bill, but it is common to leave small change or round up the total as a gesture of appreciation for good service. For example, leaving one or two euros at a café or a bit more at a restaurant is perfectly acceptable. If dining with locals or being hosted in someone's home, it's polite to compliment the food and offer thanks at the end of the meal "c'était délicieux" (it was delicious) or "merci pour ce repas" (thank you for the meal) are thoughtful phrases to use.

French culture values personal space and boundaries. When greeting someone you know, a light kiss on each cheek, known as "la bise," is common, though among strangers and in professional settings, a handshake is more typical. In casual public interactions, it's best to avoid loud voices or overly familiar behavior until you've established a relationship with someone. French people may seem reserved at first, but they often warm up quickly when treated with respect and friendliness.

Dress in Carcassonne is generally neat and modest. While there is no strict dress code, people tend to dress with a sense of casual elegance. Wearing clean, coordinated outfits even for everyday errands conveys a sense of self-respect and is part of local custom. When visiting religious sites such as churches or cathedrals, it's recommended to wear appropriate attire that covers shoulders and knees as a sign of respect.

Another important aspect of etiquette in Carcassonne is the strong emphasis on local identity and pride. The people of this region are deeply connected to their history, traditions, and land. You may hear locals speaking passionately about Cathar heritage, regional cuisine, or the preservation of local dialects. Expressing genuine interest in these subjects will often lead to warm conversations and unexpected insights. Asking about the story behind a dish or a local wine, or showing interest in the city's festivals and historical sites, is a wonderful way to engage with the culture.

Respect for the environment is also a growing part of local consciousness. Recycling is common, and many accommodations and shops are making efforts toward sustainability. Littering is frowned upon, and visitors are encouraged to dispose of waste properly and participate in the region's growing eco-conscious movement, especially when visiting outdoor areas like the Canal du Midi or the countryside near Lac de la Cavayère.

Finally, patience is key. Life in Carcassonne, as in much of rural and southern France, moves at a slower, more relaxed pace. Restaurants may take longer to serve meals, shops may close for extended lunch hours, and schedules may not always be precise. Rather than seeing this as an inconvenience, it's best to embrace it as part of the charm of the region. Taking your time, slowing down, and adjusting to the rhythm of local life is part of what makes a visit to Carcassonne so enriching.

By understanding and respecting the language, customs, and etiquette of Carcassonne, you'll not only navigate the city more smoothly, you'll also form deeper connections with its people, culture, and way of life. And in doing so, your experience will move from simply visiting a place to truly being welcomed into it.

Art, Music, and Local Handicrafts

Carcassonne may be most famous for its towering fortress and medieval history, but it also boasts a vibrant cultural life that goes far beyond stone walls and ancient battles. In this southern French city, art, music, and local craftsmanship thrive in the quiet corners of the Bastide, the bustling streets of the Cité, and the surrounding countryside. These creative expressions are deeply rooted in the region's Occitan heritage and continue to shape the city's identity today, offering visitors a rich and layered cultural experience.

Art in Carcassonne is both visible and subtle found in traditional galleries as well as in the architecture, signage, and decorative touches throughout the city. The old stone facades, colorful shutters, and wrought iron balconies of the Bastide are works of art in themselves. Inside the medieval Cité, the artistry is even more pronounced, with centuries-old carvings, stained glass, and frescoes that evoke the craftsmanship of the Middle Ages. Many churches and public buildings showcase religious and historical artwork, including delicate sculptures and mosaics that reveal the devotion and detail of earlier artisans.

For those interested in contemporary and fine arts, Carcassonne offers a variety of galleries and cultural centers. The Centre d'Art Contemporain Raymond Farbos in the Bastide hosts rotating exhibitions that feature both local and international artists, with works ranging from painting and photography to sculpture and mixed media. The

Musée des Beaux-Arts, located in a neoclassical mansion near Place Gambetta, houses a permanent collection of European paintings and decorative arts from the 17th to the 20th centuries. The museum also hosts temporary exhibitions and cultural events that give insight into the evolving art scene of the region.

Street art and public installations are becoming increasingly popular in Carcassonne, particularly in the Bastide. Throughout the year, visitors may come across murals, artist-decorated storefronts, and pop-up exhibitions in unlikely spaces. These modern expressions often explore themes tied to local history, environmental consciousness, and community identity. This dynamic blend of the old and new adds an unexpected richness to even a simple walk through the city.

Music is another vital thread in Carcassonne's cultural fabric. Traditional Occitan music, with its haunting melodies and distinctive rhythms, remains an important part of the city's heritage. You may hear it during local festivals, parades, or cultural celebrations, played on instruments like the boha (a kind of bagpipe), the graile (a wooden oboe), and the tambourin. The songs, often sung in the Occitan language, speak of love, war, and village life, connecting the modern listener with centuries of southern French tradition.

In the summer months, Carcassonne becomes a major destination for live music, especially during the Festival de Carcassonne. This citywide event includes performances of classical symphonies, operas, jazz concerts, and modern pop acts, many held in spectacular venues such as the open-air Théâtre Jean-Deschamps within the medieval Cité. Other smaller venues and bars across the Bastide offer live music throughout the year, from French chansons to blues and world music. The combination of intimate spaces and enthusiastic local audiences makes for an authentic and energizing experience.

Carcassonne is also a wonderful place to discover and support local artisans. The region is home to a variety of traditional crafts, many of which reflect its agricultural and rural history. In markets and boutique shops, you'll find handmade pottery, woven baskets, woodcarvings, and embroidered textiles all crafted with techniques passed down through generations. Local ceramics often feature earth tones and simple, rustic forms, while textile products may be adorned with geometric or floral patterns inspired by medieval designs.

Leather goods, including belts, bags, and sandals, are another highlight of the local artisan scene. Crafted by hand and often made with regional materials, these products are not only practical but deeply personal, representing the artistry of the maker. In some workshops, artisans are happy to share their methods or demonstrate their tools, providing an intimate look at the care and time that goes into each item.

One unique form of local craftsmanship found in Carcassonne is soap making. Natural, handcrafted soaps made with olive oil, lavender, honey, and herbs are a favorite souvenir among travelers. These soaps, often produced by small family-run operations, not only reflect the scents and textures of the region but also support the local economy and sustainable practices.

Another treasure is the artisanal food products that blur the line between culinary craft and cultural tradition. Jars of cassoulet, confits, jams made with regional fruits, and bottles of olive oil infused with local herbs can be found in specialty stores and are often beautifully packaged, making them perfect gifts or mementos. These edible crafts embody the values of slow living, authenticity, and connection to the land.

For those who want a deeper dive into the city's artistic traditions, several workshops and classes are available, offering hands-on experiences in pottery, painting, or culinary arts. These activities allow visitors to engage with the region's creative spirit in a personal and lasting way. Even a short class can provide a unique window into the skills and stories that shape local life.

In every corner of Carcassonne, from the historic walls of the Cité to the lively market squares of the Bastide, art, music, and handicrafts continue to flourish. They are not merely tourist attractions, they are living traditions that carry forward the identity of the city and its people. For travelers, embracing these expressions adds depth to the journey, turning a visit into a true cultural encounter. Whether you're admiring a painting, listening to a traditional tune, or bringing home a handmade keepsake, you'll carry with you a piece of Carcassonne's creative soul.

CHAPTER 6

LANDMARKS AND MUST-SEE ATTRACTIONS

Cité de Carcassonne: The Walled Fortress

The Cité de Carcassonne is not only the crown jewel of the city, it is one of the most awe-inspiring medieval sites in all of Europe. Rising above the River Aude and visible from miles away, this immense walled fortress seems as though it has stepped straight out of a storybook. With its double ring of thick stone walls, 52 watchtowers, winding cobblestone lanes, and fairytale turrets, the Cité captures the imagination of every visitor. Its dramatic silhouette and romantic atmosphere make it the number one must-see attraction in Carcassonne and the very reason many people journey to this corner of southern France.

The origins of the Cité go back more than two thousand years. The site was first occupied by the Romans in the 1st century BCE, who recognized its strategic value atop a hill overlooking the surrounding plains. They built the first defensive walls, some of which still survive today, forming the inner rampart of the current fortress. During the Middle Ages, Carcassonne flourished as a military stronghold and economic hub, especially during the 12th and 13th centuries when it became a center of Cathar resistance against the Catholic Church. The fortress played a pivotal role during the Albigensian Crusade, when the Catholic forces sought to eradicate the Cathar heresy from southern France. After the region was brought under royal control, the Cité was heavily fortified and became part of the defensive line protecting the French kingdom from the Spanish crown.

Despite its strategic importance in the Middle Ages, the Cité eventually lost its military significance. By the 19th century, it had fallen into a state of disrepair and was even scheduled for demolition. Fortunately, architect Eugène Viollet-le-Duc led a massive restoration project that revived the fortress to its former grandeur, albeit with some imaginative interpretations of medieval architecture. Today, the Cité is a UNESCO World Heritage Site and a masterpiece of historical preservation.

Visiting the Cité de Carcassonne is like stepping into the past. As you enter through one of the main gates most likely the Narbonne Gate you are immediately surrounded by soaring towers, thick ramparts, and a labyrinth of narrow lanes. The Narbonne Gate itself is an impressive structure flanked by two tall towers and accessed by a drawbridge over a dry moat. Walking through its vaulted entrance, you'll feel as though you're entering a medieval stronghold brimming with secrets.

Inside the fortress, there is much to explore. One of the highlights is the Château Comtal, the Count's Castle, located at the heart of the Cité. This 12th-century castle within a fortress offers a glimpse into the military and noble life of the Middle Ages. Visitors can explore the castle walls, tour the interior rooms and courtyards, and walk along the ramparts for breathtaking panoramic views of the city, countryside, and the Pyrenees Mountains in the distance. The rampart walk is especially recommended, as it allows you to appreciate the scale and design of the fortifications up close.

Another key site within the Cité is the Basilique Saint-Nazaire, a Gothic-Romanesque church dating back to the 11th century. Often overshadowed by the fortress walls, the basilica is a peaceful and deeply moving place. Its stained-glass windows are among the finest in southern France, casting colorful light onto the stone floors and pillars. The combination of Romanesque solidity and Gothic grace makes it a favorite for lovers of architecture and sacred spaces.

While the Cité is certainly a historical site, it is not a museum frozen in time. It is very much alive, with restaurants, cafés, artisan shops, and small hotels nestled among its winding alleys. While some parts can feel touristy during peak season, it is still possible to find quiet moments—especially early in the morning or later in the evening when the crowds thin and the golden light casts a magical glow on the stone walls.

The Cité is particularly atmospheric at night. Once the day visitors have left, the fortress takes on a more intimate and mystical character. Many visitors choose to dine within its walls after sunset or take an evening stroll along the ramparts when the towers are beautifully illuminated. Some areas of the outer walls are accessible without tickets, allowing you to enjoy the ambiance at your leisure.

To fully appreciate the Cité, consider taking a guided tour. Knowledgeable guides can share the complex history, legends, and architectural details that are easy to overlook on your own. Audio guides and pamphlets are also available at the entrance of the Château Comtal for those who prefer a self-guided experience.

For photographers, the Cité offers countless opportunities. Sunrise and sunset are particularly rewarding times to capture the golden tones of the stone walls and the dramatic interplay of light and shadow. The best views of the entire fortress can often be found from across the River Aude, especially from the old bridge, Pont Vieux, or from the scenic path along the riverbank.

Whether you're fascinated by medieval warfare, enchanted by Gothic cathedrals, or simply drawn to the romance of a bygone era, the Cité de Carcassonne will leave a deep impression. It is not just a monument, it is a symbol of the region's resilience, artistry, and layered history. Spending time here allows you to walk in the footsteps of knights, heretics, kings, and visionaries, and to lose yourself in a place where the past is still very much present.

Château Comtal and Ramparts Walk

Nestled deep within the fortified walls of the Cité de Carcassonne lies the Château Comtal, or Count's Castle, one of the most captivating features of the entire medieval complex. More than just a castle, the Château Comtal is a gateway into the military, political, and architectural history of Carcassonne. This fortified residence, surrounded by a dry moat and protected by its own defensive walls, gives visitors a vivid look at the heart of the fortress and provides direct access to the ramparts walk, an unforgettable experience that offers breathtaking views and a deeper understanding of medieval fortification.

Built in the 12th century by the Trencavel family, the Château Comtal served as the residence and stronghold of the viscounts who ruled Carcassonne. Over the centuries, it was expanded, strengthened, and later restored during the extensive 19th-century renovation led by Eugène Viollet-le-Duc. This restoration brought many of the castle's towers, walls, and interiors back to life, blending historical accuracy with elements of architectural imagination. Today, the castle serves as a museum and central feature of the Cité, drawing thousands of visitors each year.

Entry to the Château Comtal is ticketed, and while the outer areas of the Cité are free to explore, accessing the castle and the ramparts walk requires admission. The experience is well worth it. Upon entering the château, visitors pass through a drawbridge and arched gate into a courtyard flanked by stone walls, towers, and staircases that lead to various sections of the fortress. Interpretive displays and exhibits throughout the complex explain the history of Carcassonne, its Cathar past, medieval architecture, and the methods used in its fortification.

Inside the castle, you can explore rooms that once housed noble families, including small chapels, ceremonial halls, and storage areas, many of which contain fragments of stone carvings, sculptures, and architectural relics. One of the most interesting exhibits includes models and illustrations showing how Carcassonne evolved over the centuries, giving visitors a clear sense of the city's growth and the constant need for fortification and defense.

From the interior of the Château Comtal, stairways lead directly to the ramparts, arguably the most thrilling part of the visit. The ramparts of

Carcassonne form a double ring around the old city, with the inner walls dating back to Roman times and the outer defenses constructed during the Middle Ages. Walking along the ramparts places you quite literally in the footsteps of guards, soldiers, and sentinels who once patrolled the perimeter, watching for signs of attack.

The views from the ramparts are nothing short of spectacular. On one side, you can gaze out across the red-tiled rooftops of the Bastide Saint-Louis, with the Aude River winding through the landscape below. On the other side, you see the rolling hills of the Languedoc countryside and, on clear days, the distant peaks of the Pyrenees Mountains. The perspective offered from the top of the towers and walls reveals not only the scale of Carcassonne's defenses but also its strategic importance across the centuries.

As you continue along the ramparts, you'll pass a series of towers, each with its own features and history. Some are open for exploration, offering spiral staircases, arrow slits, and small chambers that once served as lookout points or guard posts. These towers provide excellent photo opportunities and moments of reflection, allowing you to imagine life in a time when Carcassonne was both a home and a battlefield.

One particularly memorable stretch of the ramparts connects the Château Comtal to the Narbonnaise Gate, Carcassonne's grand eastern entrance. This elevated passageway offers one of the most complete and scenic walks within the fortress, combining views of the gate's massive towers with sweeping panoramas of the surrounding region. Walking this route at different times of day reveals changing light and shadow that bring the ancient stones to life in new ways.

The ramparts walk can take anywhere from 30 minutes to over an hour, depending on how thoroughly you explore the various sections and towers. It's advisable to wear comfortable footwear, as the paths can be uneven and involve several staircases. Visiting early in the morning or late in the afternoon can help you avoid crowds and enjoy a more serene experience.

For those with a deeper interest in medieval military architecture, the ramparts and the Château Comtal offer valuable insight into the layered design of fortifications, the logic behind double walls, and the interplay between offense and defense in medieval times. The ability to see the layout of the city and the walls from above enhances your understanding of how Carcassonne was designed to withstand siege and how it functioned as a living, breathing community.

The combination of the Château Comtal and the ramparts walk is a must for any visitor to Carcassonne. It provides not only a visually stunning experience but also an emotional connection to the city's complex and often turbulent history. From the echo of your footsteps on ancient stones to the wind brushing against your face as you gaze over centuries-old battlements, the experience is both humbling and unforgettable. These walls have witnessed the rise and fall of empires, the lives of nobles and commoners, and the march of armies. To walk them is to be part of that enduring story.

Basilica of Saints Nazarius and Celsus

Tucked within the fortified walls of the Cité de Carcassonne lies one of the city's most cherished spiritual and architectural treasures, the Basilica of Saints Nazarius and Celsus. Often simply referred to as the Basilica of Saint-Nazaire, this sacred space is far more than just a stop on a sightseeing tour. It is a place where centuries of history, faith, and artistry converge in quiet harmony. Though it may not command the same attention as the towering ramparts or the Château Comtal, it leaves a lasting impression on visitors with its peaceful atmosphere, soaring stonework, and extraordinary stained-glass windows.

The origins of the basilica trace back to the 6th century, though the current structure was largely built between the 11th and 14th centuries. Originally constructed in Romanesque style, the church underwent significant Gothic additions in the 13th century, resulting in the harmonious blend of architectural styles that can still be seen today. It was Pope Urban II who consecrated the original church in 1096 during his travels through the region, marking its early significance within both the spiritual and civic life of Carcassonne.

The basilica was originally the cathedral of Carcassonne until 1803, when the seat of the bishopric was moved to the Bastide's Saint-Michel Cathedral. In 1898, it was granted the honorary status of a minor basilica by Pope Leo XIII. Despite this shift in prominence, the Basilica of Saint-Nazaire remains a deeply beloved site among locals and travelers alike, appreciated for its intimate beauty and solemn grace.

Approaching the basilica, you'll notice the contrast between the sturdy Romanesque nave and the more delicate Gothic elements, especially in the apse and transept. The Romanesque portions are heavy and solid, marked by rounded arches and thick walls that reflect the fortress-like sensibilities of early medieval architecture. In contrast, the Gothic additions are airier, with pointed arches, ribbed vaults, and intricate stone tracery that lift the eye heavenward and create a sense of spiritual lightness.

Step inside, and you are immediately enveloped by a hush that seems to transcend time. The cool air, dim lighting, and faint scent of old stone create a serene atmosphere perfect for quiet reflection. The long nave, lined with simple wooden pews, leads to a delicately carved choir and high altar. The juxtaposition of Romanesque solidity and Gothic elegance is striking, offering a visual narrative of architectural evolution across the centuries.

The true highlight of the basilica, however, is its stained-glass windows. Dating mostly from the 13th and 14th centuries, they are among the oldest and most beautiful in southern France. These radiant windows depict scenes from both the Old and New Testaments with remarkable detail and emotional depth. The rose window in the western façade and the lancet windows in the choir are especially breathtaking, bathing the interior in shifting patterns of colored light that change with the time of day and weather conditions. Standing in the apse and watching the morning sun illuminate scenes of saints and angels is one of the most quietly moving experiences in Carcassonne.

Along the side chapels and columns, visitors will find statues of saints, faded frescoes, and decorative carvings that speak to the devotion and craftsmanship of centuries past. Look closely at the capitals atop the columns, and you may find depictions of vines, birds, mythical creatures, and biblical scenes with small details that reward the attentive observer.

The basilica is also home to a finely carved wooden organ, which is sometimes used during religious services or concerts. If you are fortunate enough to visit when music is playing whether it's the swell of an organ or the ethereal voices of a choir the atmosphere becomes even more magical. The acoustics of the space are exquisite, carrying sound gently through the vaulted ceilings and creating an intimate, echoing resonance.

One of the basilica's most touching aspects is its continued use as a place of worship. Unlike many historic buildings that have become purely tourist sites, Saint-Nazaire remains a living religious space. Masses, weddings, and concerts are still held here, and visitors are asked to be respectful of ongoing services and the sanctity of the site. This balance between historical monument and sacred space is part of what makes the basilica so special.

Visiting the Basilica of Saints Nazarius and Celsus doesn't require a long time, but the experience stays with you. It's a place that invites you to slow down, breathe deeply, and absorb the beauty of a quieter side of Carcassonne. It reminds visitors that even in a city known for its dramatic walls and grand military history, there is also room for stillness, reverence, and the enduring power of faith expressed through stone and light.

For those interested in history, architecture, or spirituality, the basilica is an essential stop. It offers a moving contrast to the fortress walls that surround it soft where they are strong, silent where they are commanding. As you leave its peaceful interior and step back into the bustling lanes of the Cité, you'll carry with you a sense of calm and a deeper connection to the layered soul of Carcassonne.

Bastide Saint-Louis: The Lower Town

While the medieval Cité de Carcassonne often steals the spotlight, no visit to the city is truly complete without exploring Bastide Saint-Louis, the vibrant and historically rich lower town located just across the River Aude. Often overlooked by visitors who focus only on the hilltop fortress, the Bastide offers a strikingly different experience: one that reveals the rhythms of everyday life, the charm of 18th-century architecture, bustling local markets, and a sense of authenticity that gives Carcassonne its true character.

Founded in 1247 by King Louis IX (Saint Louis), the Bastide was established as a planned town during a period when the French crown sought to extend its authority over the newly annexed region after the Albigensian Crusade. The grid-like street layout unusual for medieval towns was designed to be functional, orderly, and easy to navigate. The town quickly became a center of trade, commerce, and civic life, flourishing alongside the fortified Cité, yet remaining distinct in both style and purpose.

The heart of the Bastide Saint-Louis is Place Carnot, a lively square that serves as a gathering place for both locals and visitors. Flanked by cafés, shops, and historic façades, the square is home to the weekly market, held every Tuesday, Thursday, and Saturday. On market days, the space fills with colorful stalls selling fresh produce, regional cheeses, olives, honey, cured meats, and handmade goods. The atmosphere is festive yet relaxed, and wandering among the vendors is a delightful way to discover the flavors and personalities of the region. A central fountain, dedicated to the Roman emperor Neptune, adds a touch of classical elegance to the square.

Radiating out from Place Carnot are a network of narrow streets and shaded alleys lined with 17th- and 18th-century townhouses. Their pastel-colored shutters, wrought-iron balconies, and ivy-covered walls give the Bastide a warm and inviting character. Many of these buildings now house independent boutiques, artisan shops, galleries, wine cellars, and traditional bakeries, offering a different kind of exploration than the fortress above. Here, you'll find no souvenir stalls or themed restaurants, but rather a sense of place rooted in community and local pride.

One of the architectural highlights of the Bastide is the Église Saint-Vincent, a striking Gothic church with a soaring bell tower that offers panoramic views over the rooftops of Carcassonne. Climbing the tower's spiral staircase rewards visitors with a breathtaking perspective of the entire city, from the distant mountains to the towering walls of the Cité. Inside the church, you'll find stained-glass windows, religious artwork, and a peaceful interior that reflects the spiritual life of the lower town.

Nearby, the Halle aux Grains, or old grain market, now functions as a cultural venue and event space. Originally used to store and trade grain, the building has been repurposed to host concerts, exhibitions, and community gatherings. Its transformation from economic center to cultural hub reflects the Bastide's evolution into a space that values both heritage and contemporary creativity.

The Bastide also features several small squares, each with its own charm and rhythm. Place de la République and Place Eggenfelden (named after Carcassonne's German twin town) offer quieter spots to relax with a coffee or watch the world go by. Tree-lined boulevards surrounding the Bastide mark the boundaries of the old city walls, most of which were dismantled in the 19th century to allow for expansion. Today, these boulevards are pleasant for walking or cycling, connecting the Bastide to nearby neighborhoods and the Canal du Midi.

One of the most enchanting experiences in the Bastide is simply wandering without a set destination. You might stumble upon a tucked-away courtyard filled with jasmine and geraniums, discover a tiny wine bar pouring local vintages, or find a contemporary art gallery displaying the works of a local painter. Unlike the Cité, which often feels like a living museum, the Bastide is where daily life unfolds. Children play in the squares, residents greet each other at the boulangerie, and dogs lounge in the sun beside café tables.

The contrast between the two halves of Carcassonne medieval hilltop stronghold and vibrant lower town creates a compelling dynamic. While the Cité represents the city's dramatic past and architectural grandeur, the Bastide Saint-Louis offers a glimpse into its soul. This is where you'll find the rhythm of real life, shaped by centuries of trade, resilience, and quiet evolution.

For travelers seeking a deeper and more balanced experience of Carcassonne, the Bastide is essential. It provides the warmth and nuance that rounds out the city's story, reminding visitors that Carcassonne is not just a destination frozen in time, but a living, breathing community with a rich past and a vibrant present. Whether you come to shop at the market, admire the architecture, or simply enjoy a slow lunch in the sun, the Bastide Saint-Louis welcomes you with understated elegance and timeless charm.

CHAPTER 7

OUTDOOR ADVENTURES

Walking and Cycling the Canal du Midi

One of the most rewarding ways to explore the serene beauty of Carcassonne and its surroundings is by walking or cycling along the Canal du Midi. This historic waterway, recognized as a UNESCO World Heritage Site, meanders gracefully through southern France, offering a peaceful contrast to the imposing stone walls of the Cité. Lined with centuries-old plane trees, quaint locks, stone bridges, and charming villages, the canal is not just a feat of engineering but a haven for outdoor enthusiasts seeking tranquility, nature, and authentic regional charm.

Commissioned in the 17th century by Pierre-Paul Riquet, the Canal du Midi was originally constructed to link the Atlantic Ocean to the Mediterranean Sea, thereby avoiding the long and treacherous route around the Iberian Peninsula. Stretching over 240 kilometers, the canal passes through some of the most picturesque parts of the Occitanie region, with Carcassonne serving as one of its most notable stops. The canal itself is a masterpiece of design, with a system of locks, aqueducts, tunnels, and towpaths that have been carefully preserved and are now used primarily for leisure.

In Carcassonne, the canal flows just north of the Bastide Saint-Louis and is easily accessible on foot or by bike. The shaded towpath that runs alongside the water is a favorite among locals and visitors alike. It provides a flat, well-maintained route ideal for a casual stroll, a leisurely bike ride, or a more ambitious day-long adventure. Whether you're an early riser looking to enjoy the golden morning light or a sunset lover who wants to catch the reflections of the plane trees in the water, the Canal du Midi offers a peaceful setting in all seasons.

Walking along the canal is an excellent way to slow down and appreciate the natural beauty of the region. The path winds through leafy stretches where you can listen to birdsong, watch boats drift slowly past, and observe the rhythm of rural life. Benches and grassy banks provide perfect spots for a picnic or a quiet moment of reflection. You might pass fishermen casting their lines, families enjoying an afternoon outing, or solo travelers immersed in the calming ambiance of the water.

For cyclists, the Canal du Midi is a dream route. Bicycle rentals are readily available in Carcassonne, with several rental shops offering hourly, daily, or even multi-day options. Many visitors choose to ride westward toward the village of Trèbes, a charming riverside town about 8 kilometers away, known for its lovely cafés, waterside terraces, and picturesque locks. This route is mostly shaded and traffic-free, making it suitable for cyclists of all ages and experience levels. Along the way, you'll pass vineyards, sunflower fields, and stone farmhouses that capture the essence of the French countryside.

If you're feeling more ambitious, you can continue farther along the canal to explore other towns and attractions. To the east, the path leads toward Marseillette and beyond, eventually reaching

Narbonne and the Mediterranean coast. To the west, it connects to Castelnaudary, famous for its hearty cassoulet and scenic harbor. Many of these routes are perfect for a half-day or full-day cycling excursion, with plenty of opportunities to stop, explore, and enjoy the local cuisine along the way.

The canal also offers cultural interest, especially at the locks, where you can watch the lock-keepers guide boats through the water levels. Some of the lock houses have been transformed into small cafés or artisan shops, where you can take a break and learn more about the canal's history. Interpretive signs along the route provide insights into the engineering, construction, and impact of this incredible project that once revolutionized trade in France.

Spring and autumn are ideal seasons for walking and cycling the Canal du Midi, thanks to mild temperatures and fewer tourists. Summer, while warmer, brings lush greenery and lively boat traffic, adding to the atmosphere. Winter is quieter, but the bare trees reveal more of the canal's architectural features and the gentle stillness of the season can be quite enchanting.

For those who prefer a guided experience, several local tour operators offer canal-focused excursions that combine biking with wine tastings, heritage visits, or even barge rides. These tours often include detailed commentary on the canal's history and the surrounding region, enriching your adventure with stories and local knowledge.

Regardless of how far you go or how fast you travel, the Canal du Midi offers a deeply satisfying escape from the busy pace of urban sightseeing. It allows you to connect with nature, breathe in the fresh countryside air, and discover a quieter side of Carcassonne that many visitors miss. Whether you walk a short stretch at sunrise or spend a full day cycling through vineyards and villages, the experience is both grounding and memorable.

The Canal du Midi isn't just a route through southern France, it's a journey through time, landscape, and local life. It invites you to pause, observe, and absorb the gentle beauty that defines this enchanting part of the world.

Wine Tours and Vineyard Excursions

Carcassonne is more than a medieval marvel; it is also a gateway to one of the most dynamic and historically rich wine regions in France. Surrounded by rolling hills, sun-drenched vineyards, and ancient winemaking traditions, the area offers a wealth of opportunities for travelers who want to explore the world of wine beyond the glass. Wine tours and vineyard excursions are among the most rewarding outdoor adventures in the region, combining scenic beauty, cultural discovery, and sensory delight in a uniquely southern French experience.

The area around Carcassonne falls within the Languedoc wine region, one of the largest and most diverse wine-producing areas in the world. This region has been cultivating vines since Roman times, and its centuries-old expertise is reflected in the quality and variety of wines it produces today. From robust reds to crisp whites and delicate rosés, the wines of Languedoc and particularly those in the Aude department where Carcassonne is located offer something for every palate.

Many of the vineyards near Carcassonne are small, family-owned domaines that welcome visitors with warmth and authenticity. A typical wine tour begins with a scenic drive or bike ride through vine-covered landscapes, dotted with stone farmhouses and medieval villages. Upon arriving at a vineyard, you'll often be greeted by the winemaker or a knowledgeable staff member who will guide you through the property, explain the grape varieties, and walk you through the winemaking process. You'll learn about terroir the unique combination of soil, climate, and elevation that shapes the flavor profile of the wine and gain insight into the region's winemaking philosophy.

One of the most popular nearby wine appellations is Minervois, located just north of Carcassonne. This area is known for its robust red blends, often made with Syrah, Grenache, and Mourvèdre. The landscape is rugged and beautiful, with vineyards carved into hillsides and ancient ruins dotting the countryside. Another nearby appellation is Corbières, southwest of the city, which offers a broad range of reds and whites with bold character and complex aromas. Limoux, to the south, is famous for producing some of the oldest sparkling wines in France predating Champagne with styles ranging from dry and crisp to creamy and aromatic.

Visiting these vineyards provides more than just a tasting. It's an immersive experience that often includes a guided tour of the cellars, barrel rooms, and bottling facilities. Many vineyards are housed in centuries-old stone buildings with vaulted ceilings and rustic charm, creating an atmosphere that feels timeless and deeply rooted. As you walk through rows of aging barrels or stainless-steel fermentation tanks, you begin to understand the care, patience, and craftsmanship that go into every bottle.

The highlight of any vineyard excursion is, of course, the tasting. Seated in a shaded courtyard, rustic tasting room, or terrace overlooking the vines, you'll sample a range of wines accompanied by expert explanations of their origins, tasting notes, and suggested pairings. Many tastings are accompanied by local snacks such as cheese, charcuterie, olives, or tapenade, further connecting you to the flavors of the region. The pace is unhurried, encouraging conversation, reflection, and a deep appreciation for the wine and its story.

For those looking for a more comprehensive outing, full-day wine tours from Carcassonne are available through local tour operators. These tours often include visits to multiple vineyards across different appellations, a gourmet lunch at a countryside inn or vineyard restaurant, and transportation so you can enjoy the wines without worry. Some even include cultural stops at nearby castles, abbeys, or market towns, blending wine appreciation with historical exploration.

If you prefer to explore independently, many vineyards allow drop-in visits or offer appointments for small groups. The tourist offices in Carcassonne and the surrounding towns can provide maps, recommendations, and contact details for various wineries, along with tips on the best times to visit. Spring and autumn are ideal seasons for wine touring, offering pleasant weather, fewer crowds, and, in autumn, the beautiful sight of grape harvest and golden foliage.

For a unique experience, some vineyards also offer hands-on workshops where you can try blending your own wine, take part in seasonal activities like grape picking or pruning, or learn the basics of wine and food pairing. These workshops provide a deeper understanding of the winemaker's art and often come with a bottle of your own creation to take home.

No matter your level of wine knowledge, from curious beginner to seasoned connoisseur, a wine tour in the Carcassonne region is a deeply enriching adventure. It's a chance to step out of the city, breathe in the lavender-scented countryside, and connect with a tradition that defines much of the local identity and economy. It also offers the simple pleasure of sipping excellent wine in the place where it was born, surrounded by the very vines that produced it.

When the day ends and you return to Carcassonne, perhaps with a few bottles tucked under your arm, you'll carry with you not just the taste of the wine, but the stories, landscapes, and people behind it. Wine in this region is not just a drink, it's a celebration of place, time, and the enduring connection between the land and those who tend it. A vineyard excursion is more than a highlight of your trip; it's an invitation to savor the essence of southern France, one glass at a time.

Day Trips to the Pyrenees and Cathar Castles

For travelers seeking to enrich their Carcassonne experience with awe-inspiring landscapes and deep historical intrigue, few adventures compare to a day trip to the nearby Pyrenees Mountains and the legendary Cathar Castles. These excursions offer a remarkable contrast to the walled city, taking you into the heart of a region shaped by dramatic geography, spiritual resilience, and centuries of conflict. Whether you're drawn to hiking scenic mountain trails or uncovering the mysteries of medieval strongholds perched on cliffs, these destinations promise a day of unforgettable discovery.

The Pyrenees, forming a natural border between France and Spain, are located just a couple of hours south of Carcassonne by car. As you venture into these ancient mountains, the landscape shifts dramatically rolling vineyards and farmland give way to soaring peaks, forested valleys, and clear rushing streams. The fresh mountain air, cooler temperatures, and breathtaking vistas make this region a paradise for nature lovers and outdoor adventurers.

Several hiking trails in the foothills and lower slopes of the Pyrenees are accessible on a day trip from Carcassonne. These range from leisurely forest walks to more demanding treks that climb into alpine meadows with panoramic views. The Aude Valley and Pays de Sault offer particularly beautiful routes, with well-marked paths through pine woods and wildflower-filled clearings. Birdwatchers, photographers, and those simply seeking a tranquil escape from the city will find this area especially rewarding.

But beyond the natural beauty of the Pyrenees lies a captivating historical layer: the Cathar legacy. The Cathars were a religious group that flourished in the Languedoc region during the 12th and 13th centuries. Their beliefs, which diverged significantly from those of the Catholic Church, were eventually declared heretical. The resulting Albigensian Crusade a brutal campaign led by the Church and the French crown led to the persecution and near-eradication of the Cathars. In response, they built and sought refuge in remote mountaintop castles, many of which still stand today in haunting ruin.

These Cathar Castles, often referred to as "les citadelles du vertige" (castles of vertigo), are among the most striking historical sites in France. Perched atop craggy cliffs and steep escarpments, they are not only architectural wonders but also monuments to defiance and spiritual conviction. Visiting them requires a spirit of adventure, as reaching many of these sites involves a short hike or climb—but the reward is immense.

One of the most iconic Cathar castles is Château de Peyrepertuse. Located about two hours from Carcassonne, this sprawling ruin is set high on a limestone ridge and offers panoramic views across the Corbières mountains. Once a powerful fortress, it is often compared to a stone ship sailing above the clouds. Walking along its ramparts and imagining the Cathars who once took refuge there is a powerful and moving experience.

Nearby, Château de Quéribus stands like a sentinel on the edge of a rocky peak. Though smaller than Peyrepertuse, Quéribus is no less dramatic. It was one of the last Cathar strongholds to fall during the Crusade and remains a symbol of their enduring resistance. From its lookout tower, you can see deep into the valleys below and even glimpse the distant Pyrenees peaks on a clear day.

Other Cathar sites accessible from Carcassonne include Château de Puilaurens, nestled in the forested mountains near Lapradelle, and Château de Montségur, perhaps the most famous of all. Montségur was the site of a tragic siege in 1244, where over 200 Cathars were burned at the stake after refusing to renounce their faith. The site, reached by a steep trail, exudes a solemn and sacred energy. Visiting Montségur is not only a physical journey but an emotional one—an encounter with one of the darkest and most poignant chapters in the region's past.

For a more structured experience, guided tours from Carcassonne are available and often include transport, historical commentary, and stops at multiple castle sites. These tours offer context and insight that enrich the visit, especially for those unfamiliar with Cathar history. Alternatively, renting a car allows for a more flexible itinerary, letting you explore at your own pace and discover hidden gems along the way, such as quiet villages, vineyard views, and riverside picnic spots.

Packing a day bag for a Cathar castle or Pyrenees excursion should include good walking shoes, water, sun protection, and a camera. While some sites have small visitor centers or kiosks, others are completely unstaffed, so it's wise to bring a map or GPS device and plan your route in advance. Weather in the mountains can change quickly, so dressing in layers is also recommended.

A day trip to the Pyrenees and the Cathar Castles is more than just a scenic outing; it's a journey into the soul of Occitanie. These landscapes and ruins hold stories of courage, faith, and survival that continue to resonate today. The sense of standing where rebels once stood, overlooking valleys unchanged by time, offers both reflection and inspiration.

By venturing beyond Carcassonne's walls to explore these extraordinary places, travelers gain a deeper understanding of the region's richness not only in its physical beauty but in its spiritual and historical depth. It's an adventure that lingers in the memory long after the castles fade into the mist.

CHAPTER 8

SMART TRAVEL TIPS

Safety and Health Essentials

Traveling to Carcassonne is a rewarding experience filled with discovery, charm, and rich history, but like any destination, it's important to prepare with safety and health in mind. Though Carcassonne is generally considered a safe and welcoming place for travelers, understanding the basic precautions and having practical information can ensure a smooth, stress-free journey. From emergency contacts to health tips and personal safety practices, this section provides essential guidance to help you feel confident and secure throughout your visit.

Carcassonne, like most French cities, maintains a relatively low crime rate, especially in the heavily touristed areas such as the Cité and Bastide Saint-Louis. Violent crime is extremely rare. However, petty theft, particularly pickpocketing, can occur during busy seasons or in crowded areas. Travelers are encouraged to keep their personal belongings secure. Avoid keeping valuables in easily accessible pockets or bags, especially when walking through popular squares or riding public transport. Anti-theft backpacks or crossbody bags that can be worn close to the body are useful and discreet ways to carry essentials.

While walking through the Cité de Carcassonne or any narrow alleyways, keep an eye on your surroundings, especially during peak tourist months. Although the fortress feels like a fairy-tale village, it can become quite crowded, making it easier for opportunists to operate unnoticed. Always be mindful of your personal belongings in restaurants, cafés, and public seating areas, and avoid leaving your phone or bag on the table or a chair unattended.

In terms of health care, Carcassonne has several pharmacies and medical centers that are well-equipped to handle minor illnesses, injuries, or consultations. Pharmacies are easily identifiable by their green neon crosses and are typically open Monday through Saturday, with a rotating schedule of emergency pharmacies available at night or on Sundays. Pharmacists in France are knowledgeable and can often provide over-the-counter remedies or refer you to a doctor if needed.

For more serious medical needs, the Centre Hospitalier de Carcassonne, located in the Ville Basse (Lower Town), is a modern facility offering emergency services. The emergency number in France is 112, which connects you to all emergency services including medical, fire, and police. If you require a non-emergency medical appointment, you can often schedule a consultation through your hotel or by visiting a local medical center. Travelers from EU countries can use their European Health Insurance Card (EHIC), while visitors from outside the EU should ensure they have adequate travel health insurance before departure.

Drinking water in Carcassonne is safe and widely available. You can refill your bottle from public fountains unless otherwise marked, and tap water is provided freely in restaurants if requested. During the warmer months, particularly in July and August, staying hydrated is essential as temperatures can rise significantly, especially when walking long distances or exploring sun-exposed landmarks like the ramparts.

France does not require any specific vaccinations for travel, but it's always wise to be up to date on routine immunizations such as tetanus, measles, and hepatitis A. If you're planning on engaging in outdoor activities like hiking, especially in the Pyrenees or countryside, insect repellent is advisable to protect against ticks and mosquitoes. Though the risk of tick-borne illness is low, proper precautions can prevent discomfort or complications.

Sun protection is another health priority, especially if you'll be spending time outdoors exploring the Cité, cycling along the Canal du Midi, or touring vineyards. Sunscreen, a wide-brimmed hat, and sunglasses will help protect you from the strong southern French sun, particularly in late spring through early autumn. Consider wearing breathable clothing and taking breaks in shaded areas to avoid heat exhaustion.

If you have dietary restrictions or food allergies, be proactive when dining out. While many restaurants in Carcassonne are accommodating, it's helpful to learn a few key phrases in French to explain your needs, or to carry a written explanation if the allergy is severe. Many establishments will do their best to adapt meals, especially in the more tourist-savvy parts of the city.

As for transportation safety, both public and private options in Carcassonne are reliable. Buses are punctual and generally safe, and taxis or rideshare services are available for late-night travel. If you're cycling or walking around town, be cautious on roads shared with vehicles. Always use designated paths when available, and wear visible clothing if traveling early in the morning or after dusk.

Finally, keeping digital backups of your travel documents, passport, insurance, accommodation details, and transport tickets is a wise precaution. Store them securely online or in a password-protected app. Carrying a photocopy of your passport can also be helpful if the original is lost or stolen.

With just a bit of forethought and preparation, you'll find Carcassonne to be a safe, clean, and health-conscious destination. The city welcomes visitors warmly, and with these safety and health essentials in place, you'll be free to immerse yourself in its medieval wonders, outdoor beauty, and culinary delights with confidence and peace of mind.

Packing Tips and Local Etiquette

When preparing for a trip to Carcassonne, thoughtful packing and an understanding of local etiquette can make your journey more enjoyable and respectful. Whether you're wandering through cobblestone streets, exploring the legendary fortress, or sharing a meal with locals, having the right items in your luggage and the right attitude in your interactions will ensure a smooth and culturally enriching experience. Carcassonne's climate, terrain, and social customs all play a role in determining what you should bring and how to behave while visiting.

Carcassonne experiences a Mediterranean climate, meaning hot, dry summers and mild, damp winters. Packing should reflect seasonal variations. If you're visiting between May and September, prepare for warm to hot temperatures, especially in July and August when daytime highs often exceed 30°C (86°F). Lightweight, breathable clothing is essential for staying comfortable. Opt for cotton or linen shirts, shorts or skirts, and a wide-brimmed hat to protect yourself from the strong southern sun. Don't forget sunscreen and sunglasses to shield your skin and eyes during outdoor activities like walking the ramparts, cycling the Canal du Midi, or touring vineyards.

Comfortable walking shoes are a must year-round. The medieval streets of the Cité de Carcassonne are paved with cobblestones, and exploring the city often involves climbing steps or navigating uneven paths. Choose sturdy shoes with good grip, especially if you plan to visit Cathar castles or take day hikes in the Pyrenees. During autumn and winter, weather can be cooler and wetter, so include a waterproof jacket, layers such as sweaters or fleeces, and possibly an umbrella. Winters are rarely harsh, but evening temperatures can drop significantly.

Packing a small daypack is also a good idea. It's useful for carrying water, snacks, guidebooks, a camera, or an extra layer as you explore. A reusable water bottle will come in handy, as the tap water in Carcassonne is safe to drink and public fountains are available throughout the city. Also consider bringing a power adapter for French electrical outlets (Type C or E, 230V). If you're relying on mobile devices or cameras, a portable charger can be useful for long days out.

Aside from practical items, you'll also want to bring a few dressier outfits if you plan to dine in fine restaurants or attend cultural events like concerts at the Château Comtal or in local churches. While the atmosphere in Carcassonne is generally casual, the French appreciate neat and respectful attire, especially in the evenings. Avoid overly casual clothing like gym wear or beach flip-flops when dining out.

Understanding local etiquette will enhance your interactions and show respect for the culture. French people tend to value politeness and formal greetings. When entering a shop, restaurant, or even a small market stall, it's customary to greet the vendor with a simple "Bonjour" during the day or "Bonsoir" in the evening. Failing to do so can be seen as rude, even if unintentional. When leaving, a polite "Merci, au revoir" is equally appreciated.

In restaurants, table manners are important. It's customary to wait for everyone to be served before starting to eat, and to keep your hands visible on the table but not resting in your lap. Tipping is not mandatory in France as service is typically included in the bill, but rounding up or leaving small change for good service is a thoughtful gesture. In cafés or casual bistros, a tip of one to two euros is common.

If you're invited into someone's home, even for a casual gathering, it's polite to bring a small gift such as flowers, a bottle of wine, or a box of local chocolates. Punctuality is appreciated, so try to be on time. During conversation, avoid overly personal topics unless invited to discuss them, and keep your tone friendly and respectful. The French tend to appreciate thoughtful conversation and moderate volume in public settings.

When visiting historical or religious sites such as the Basilica of Saints Nazarius and Celsus, dress modestly and behave respectfully. Silence or low voices are expected inside churches, especially if services are in progress. Photography may be restricted in certain areas, so always look for signs or ask permission before taking photos.

In terms of sustainability, France encourages responsible tourism. Avoid single-use plastics, recycle when possible, and support local artisans and businesses rather than large chain stores. Respecting the environment and local customs not only enhances your experience but also contributes to preserving the cultural and natural heritage of the region.

Learning a few basic French phrases is another simple but powerful way to show respect. While many people in Carcassonne's tourism industry speak some English, even simple efforts like "s'il vous plaît" (please), "merci" (thank you), and "parlez-vous anglais?" (do you speak English?) go a long way in creating positive connections.

In summary, packing with purpose and practicing local etiquette will help you blend seamlessly into the rhythm of life in Carcassonne. With the right clothes, a few essential items, and a respectful approach to local culture, your visit will not only be more comfortable but also more meaningful. Whether you're hiking to a Cathar castle, sipping wine in a vineyard, or sharing a quiet moment in the Cité, thoughtful preparation ensures that every moment in Carcassonne can be fully enjoyed.

Useful Apps and Emergency Contacts

Traveling smart in Carcassonne goes beyond packing the right clothes and learning local customs; it also means knowing how to stay informed, connected, and safe. In today's digital world, having the right apps at your fingertips and being aware of essential emergency contacts can make your trip smoother and more secure. From navigating the medieval city streets to handling unexpected situations, this section offers practical guidance on how to use technology and prepare for the unexpected with confidence.

Several useful mobile apps can greatly enhance your experience in Carcassonne and throughout the Occitanie region. One of the first to download is Google Maps, which offers accurate directions whether you're walking through the maze-like alleys of the Cité or finding your way to a local vineyard. Make sure to download an offline map of the Carcassonne area before your arrival, so you can navigate even without a mobile data connection.

For public transportation, the "RTCA Carcassonne Agglo" app (Régie des Transports de Carcassonne Agglo) is helpful for checking bus schedules, planning routes, and purchasing digital tickets. Carcassonne's bus system is relatively easy to use, and this app ensures you're always aware of the nearest stop and when the next bus will arrive. You can also use SNCF Connect if you plan on taking regional trains to or from Carcassonne, such as journeys to Toulouse, Narbonne, or Limoux.

Language can sometimes be a barrier, especially in smaller shops or more rural areas. Apps like Google Translate or DeepL Translate are invaluable for real-time translation of menus, signs, or conversations. You can use the camera function to instantly translate text or type phrases you need to communicate. While many locals working in tourism speak English, showing a willingness to engage in French even with help goes a long way.

If you're planning to explore vineyards or take day trips to remote castles, having a rideshare or taxi app can be useful. While Uber and Lyft are not widely used in Carcassonne, local taxi services can often be booked through apps or by phone. G7 Taxi and Allo Taxi Carcassonne are two options to consider, and both offer websites or apps with booking capabilities.

For restaurant reservations or finding top-rated eateries, TheFork (La Fourchette) is widely used in France. You can browse reviews, see menus, make reservations, and even enjoy discounts at some establishments. TripAdvisor is another good app for checking user reviews of attractions, hotels, and tours in and around Carcassonne.

If you're interested in guided walks or exploring the region independently with a deeper sense of context, apps like Rick Steves Audio Europe or VoiceMap offer GPS-enabled audio tours. Some local tourism boards also have their own apps or self-guided tour tools that you can find through the Carcassonne Tourist Office.

Weather apps like AccuWeather or Meteo France will help you plan your days based on accurate forecasts. This is especially helpful when deciding whether to visit a hilltop Cathar castle or enjoy a boat ride on the Canal du Midi. The weather in southern France can change quickly, especially in spring or autumn, so checking conditions before setting out is always smart.

Beyond apps, it's critical to know the emergency contact numbers in France. The general emergency number is 112. This number can be dialed from any phone, mobile or landline, and will connect you to emergency services including police, fire, and medical help. It is available 24/7 and operators typically speak multiple languages, including English.

Here are the most important emergency numbers to remember:

- 112 – European emergency number (all emergencies)
- 15 – SAMU (Medical emergency services)
- 17 – Police (Police secours)
- 18 – Fire brigade (Pompiers)
- 114 – Emergency text service for people with hearing or speech impairments (SMS only)

If you lose your passport or encounter a legal issue, you should contact your country's embassy or consulate. The nearest embassies are typically located in Toulouse or Montpellier, both within a couple of hours' reach by train or car. Keep digital copies of your passport, travel insurance, medical records, and important bookings stored safely in the cloud or on your phone for easy access in case of loss or emergency.

Local health services are accessible, and pharmacies are the first place to go for minor medical needs. Most pharmacists speak some English and can recommend treatments or refer you to a doctor. If you require hospital care, Centre Hospitalier de Carcassonne is the main facility and offers emergency services. The address is 1060 Chemin de la Madeleine, and the phone number is +33 4 68 24 24 24.

Having a few key apps and knowing these essential contacts can save you time, reduce stress, and even keep you safe. While Carcassonne is a generally safe and traveler-friendly destination, being prepared with the right digital tools and emergency information means you can focus on enjoying the magic of this historic city and the adventures beyond its ancient walls.

CHAPTER 9

SAMPLE ITINERARIES

<u>One Day in Carcassonne: Highlights Tour</u>

If you only have one day to spend in Carcassonne, you can still experience the best of this remarkable city by following a thoughtfully planned itinerary that captures its medieval magic, vibrant local culture, and breathtaking scenery. While Carcassonne deserves more than a day, this highlights tour allows you to soak in its essential experiences, from walking the ancient ramparts to savoring the flavors of southern France, all within a single unforgettable day.

Begin your morning early with a walk across the Pont Vieux, the Old Bridge that spans the River Aude and links the lower town (Bastide Saint-Louis) with the upper fortified city (Cité de Carcassonne). The view from the bridge at sunrise is particularly captivating, as golden light bathes the iconic stone towers and walls of the Cité. The bridge itself, dating back to the 14th century, sets the tone for the day's journey into history.

Once across the bridge, make your way through the main gate of the Cité Porte Narbonnaise and step into a storybook world of cobbled lanes, turreted walls, and medieval atmosphere. Your first stop should be the Château Comtal, the count's castle that sits at the heart of the fortress. Allocate at least an hour to tour the castle's interiors, towers, and walkways, and don't miss the panoramic ramparts walk. The views over the rooftops of the Cité and the surrounding Aude countryside are spectacular and provide a powerful sense of Carcassonne's defensive design and its strategic importance through centuries of conflict.

After your tour of the Château, stroll through the medieval lanes of the Cité. The streets are lined with artisan shops, bookshops, and local boutiques, where you can find everything from handmade soaps to Carcassonne-themed souvenirs. Around mid-morning, take a break at one of the quiet cafés tucked into a side alley and enjoy a coffee and a traditional pastry like a croissant or pain au chocolat.

Your next stop is the Basilica of Saints Nazarius and Celsus, located within the Cité walls. This Gothic-Romanesque church features stunning stained-glass windows, some dating back to the 13th century. The peaceful atmosphere inside invites a moment of reflection amid your busy exploration. Take time to admire the intricately carved stonework and the soaring arches before stepping back into the sunlight.

As midday approaches, head to Place Marcou, the central square inside the Cité, where you'll find several restaurants offering traditional regional dishes. For an authentic experience, order cassoulet, a slow-cooked stew of white beans, duck, and sausage that originates from the region. Pair it with a glass of local Minervois or Corbières wine, and enjoy your lunch in the open air, surrounded by the stone walls of history.

After lunch, descend from the Cité and cross back over to the Bastide Saint-Louis, the lower town of Carcassonne. This part of the city offers a different, more local perspective. Begin at Place Carnot, the lively central square, and browse the stalls if you happen to be there on a market day. Even on quiet afternoons, the square is a pleasant place to sit with a drink or enjoy a bit of people-watching under the shade of the trees.

Next, visit Église Saint-Vincent, a Gothic church with a bell tower that you can climb for a panoramic view of the lower town and the distant Pyrenees. The climb is well worth the effort, offering a contrasting view to that of the Cité's ramparts and reminding you of the layers of history that coexist in Carcassonne.

If time permits, take a short walk to the Canal du Midi, a peaceful and scenic spot to unwind in the late afternoon. You might opt for a short boat ride if one is available, or simply walk along the towpath under the shade of the trees. It's a quiet, reflective counterpoint to the intensity of the medieval fortress and a perfect way to wind down the day.

As evening falls, return to the Cité for dinner, ideally at one of the restaurants offering a terrace with a view of the illuminated fortress walls. As night descends, the ramparts light up in a golden glow, casting a romantic and mystical aura over the city. Dining under the stars with the silhouette of the towers above you provides a magical ending to your day.

This one-day itinerary through Carcassonne allows you to experience the essence of the city: its grandeur, its local life, and its enduring sense of place. Though brief, your journey will leave a deep impression and a desire to return and explore more. Whether you're a history enthusiast, a culinary traveler, or simply a curious visitor, Carcassonne in one day offers an immersion into a world unlike any other.

Three-Day Itinerary: History, Food & Culture

A three-day stay in Carcassonne allows for a deeper exploration of the city's rich tapestry of medieval architecture, regional cuisine, and vibrant cultural traditions. With more time, you can move at a more relaxed pace while still covering all the essential experiences, both within the fortified walls of the Cité and in the surrounding countryside. This itinerary is perfect for travelers who want to immerse themselves in history, indulge in southern French flavors, and engage with the rhythms of local life.

Day 1: Discover the Medieval Heart of Carcassonne

Start your first day with a leisurely breakfast at a café near Place Carnot in the Bastide Saint-Louis. A croissant and café crème will provide the perfect fuel for a full day of exploration. After breakfast, make your way across the Pont Vieux for your first real encounter with the majestic Cité de Carcassonne.

Enter through the Porte Narbonnaise and allow yourself to be transported back in time. Your first major stop should be the Château Comtal, where you can tour the interior rooms, ramparts, and towers. Take your time with the self-guided or audio tour to fully absorb the historical significance of this strategic stronghold. The views from the ramparts over the Aude River and beyond to the Pyrenees are breathtaking.

After visiting the castle, wander through the narrow, cobbled lanes of the Cité. Explore the artisan shops and galleries, stopping for a light lunch at one of the restaurants tucked into a courtyard or along a side street. Cassoulet, a regional specialty, is a hearty option and a must-try dish while in Carcassonne.

In the afternoon, visit the Basilica of Saints Nazarius and Celsus. Spend some time admiring the impressive stained glass windows and Gothic details. Then, stroll around the ramparts at sunset as the light turns golden and the fortress takes on a dreamy, otherworldly glow.

Finish your day with dinner at a traditional restaurant within the Cité. Many places offer terrace seating with views of the illuminated towers, providing a magical setting to enjoy local wine and cuisine.

Day 2: Cultural Immersion and Local Life in the Bastide

Begin your second day in the Bastide Saint-Louis, the lower town of Carcassonne. This area often receives less attention than the Cité, but it offers a vibrant and authentic slice of local life. If your visit coincides with a market day (typically Tuesday, Thursday, or Saturday), head to Place Carnot where stalls brim with fresh produce, cheeses, charcuterie, baked goods, and handmade crafts.

After exploring the market, visit the Église Saint-Vincent nearby. If you're feeling adventurous, climb the bell tower for panoramic views of the city and the surrounding countryside. Then walk along the Rue de Verdun, lined with shops, bakeries, and hidden squares, and stop for lunch at a local brasserie.

In the afternoon, take a stroll to the Canal du Midi. Depending on your interests, you can enjoy a relaxing boat cruise or simply walk or bike along the peaceful towpath. The canal is a UNESCO World Heritage Site and provides a tranquil, green escape from the bustle of the city.

As evening approaches, consider attending a cultural event if one is available—Carcassonne often hosts concerts, art exhibitions, and theatrical performances, particularly in spring and summer. Alternatively, opt for a more casual night with wine tasting at a local bar or wine shop where you can sample selections from nearby vineyards in Minervois or Corbières.

Day 3: Day Trip to Cathar Country and Culinary Exploration
On your third day, venture beyond the city to explore the rugged countryside and the remnants of Cathar history. Rent a car or join a guided tour to visit one of the iconic Cathar castles—Château de Peyrepertuse or Château de Quéribus are two excellent choices. These dramatic ruins are perched on rocky peaks and offer not only historical intrigue but also stunning views of the Languedoc landscape.

If time allows, make a stop in a nearby village such as Cucugnan or Lagrasse. These charming communities offer a slower pace and are filled with stone houses, quaint shops, and inviting cafés. Plan to enjoy a leisurely lunch at a countryside inn, where you can sample rustic regional dishes made from local ingredients.

Return to Carcassonne in the late afternoon and spend your final evening savoring the culinary delights of the region. Book a table at a reputable restaurant that specializes in Languedoc cuisine and pair your meal with a bottle of local wine. Dishes like duck confit, foie gras, or a lighter seafood option provide a delicious conclusion to your stay.

If you still have energy after dinner, take a final stroll around the outer walls of the Cité. The fortress, bathed in golden light, provides a romantic and contemplative end to your three-day journey.

This itinerary balances the must-see highlights of Carcassonne with meaningful experiences that immerse you in the region's flavors, landscapes, and cultural fabric. With three days, you'll gain not just a snapshot of this extraordinary destination, but a deeper appreciation for its enduring spirit and timeless beauty.

A Week in Carcassonne and Beyond

Spending a full week in Carcassonne allows for a truly immersive experience, one where you can explore the medieval city in depth, sample the best of the local food and wine, delve into the rich history of the surrounding Cathar region, and enjoy relaxing outdoor adventures in the Occitanie countryside. With seven days at your disposal, you can blend sightseeing with leisure, and cultural exploration with culinary discovery. This itinerary offers a perfect balance of time in Carcassonne and day trips to nearby gems that enhance your understanding of the region's layered history and natural beauty.

Day 1: Arrival and First Impressions

Begin your week with a relaxed arrival and check-in at your chosen accommodation. Whether you stay inside the Cité or in the Bastide Saint-Louis, take your time settling in and familiarizing yourself with the layout of the city. Spend the afternoon walking through the narrow streets of the Cité de Carcassonne, soaking in the fairytale atmosphere and getting a feel for the medieval setting. Have dinner in one of the cozy restaurants inside the fortified walls and enjoy a glass of local wine while gazing at the towers lit up against the night sky.

Day 2: In-Depth Cité Exploration

Dedicate this day to a full exploration of the Cité. Start with a visit to the Château Comtal and take a detailed tour of its towers, inner chambers, and ramparts. Walk the entire perimeter of the fortress walls for panoramic views of the surrounding countryside. Visit the Basilica of Saints Nazarius and Celsus and spend time admiring its Gothic architecture and centuries-old stained glass windows. Stop for lunch at Place Marcou, then continue to explore the artisan shops, museums, and hidden courtyards scattered throughout the fortress. In the evening, attend a cultural event or enjoy a medieval-themed dinner.

Day 3: Bastide Saint-Louis and Canal du Midi

Today, explore the Bastide Saint-Louis, Carcassonne's lower town. Begin at Place Carnot and visit the morning market if available. Wander through the grid-like streets of the bastide, stopping at local bakeries, antique shops, and galleries. Visit Église Saint-Vincent and climb the bell tower for sweeping views. In the afternoon, walk or bike along the Canal du Midi. This peaceful UNESCO World Heritage Site offers shaded towpaths and opportunities for a short boat cruise. In the evening, enjoy dinner by the canal or in one of the local bistros tucked away on a quiet street.

Day 4: Cathar Castles Excursion

Take a day trip into the heart of Cathar country. Rent a car or join a guided tour to visit two of the most impressive Cathar castles: Château de Quéribus and Château de Peyrepertuse. These mountaintop fortresses are steeped in history and surrounded by dramatic landscapes. Bring comfortable shoes for the short but steep hikes required to reach them. Stop in the picturesque village of Cucugnan for lunch and explore its rustic charm. Return to Carcassonne in the late afternoon and spend the evening relaxing at your accommodation or enjoying a casual meal.

Day 5: Wine Tasting and Countryside Charm
Spend the fifth day indulging in the wine culture of the Languedoc region. Arrange a vineyard tour and wine tasting in Minervois, Corbières, or Limoux. Many of the domaines are family-run and offer guided tastings that include explanations of the winemaking process and pairings with local cheeses and meats. Enjoy lunch at a countryside winery or restaurant overlooking the vineyards. In the afternoon, visit the nearby town of Lagrasse, known for its medieval abbey, stone bridges, and artisan shops. It's one of France's most beautiful villages and provides a peaceful contrast to the grandeur of Carcassonne.

Day 6: Outdoor Adventure in the Pyrenees

For a change of pace, head south toward the foothills of the Pyrenees. The region offers hiking trails, riverside walks, and scenic drives through forested valleys and mountain passes. The Pays de Sault and the Plateau de Beille offer accessible hiking routes with rewarding views. You can also explore natural caves, waterfalls, and hidden lakes, depending on your level of adventure. Pack a picnic and spend the day immersed in nature. Upon returning to Carcassonne, treat yourself to a hearty regional dinner—perhaps duck confit or a dish with locally foraged mushrooms, if in season.

Day 7: Leisure and Last Discoveries

On your final day, take it slow. Revisit your favorite spots within the Cité or Bastide, do some last-minute shopping for souvenirs, and enjoy a relaxed lunch at a terrace café. If you haven't yet, visit the Museum of the Inquisition or the School Museum for a quirky historical detour. Alternatively, book a spa treatment or enjoy a peaceful moment by the canal or in a local garden. In the evening, choose a special restaurant for your farewell dinner. Watch the sunset over the ramparts one last time, reflecting on the layers of history, culture, and beauty that Carcassonne has offered throughout your week.

Spending a full week in Carcassonne and its surroundings allows you to go beyond the postcard views and truly connect with the soul of southern France. With its blend of medieval grandeur, rural tranquility, and rich gastronomic tradition, this itinerary offers a fulfilling, varied, and memorable travel experience for every kind of visitor.

CONCLUSION

Final Thoughts and Inspiration for Your Journey

As your journey through Carcassonne draws to a close, it's time to pause and reflect on the layers of history, beauty, and experience this timeless city offers. Nestled in the heart of southern France, Carcassonne is not just a destination; it's a place where legends linger in stone, where centuries whisper through cobbled lanes, and where every moment feels like a step through time. Whether you came for a brief escape or a week-long immersion, Carcassonne rewards the curious traveler with an unforgettable blend of storybook charm and grounded authenticity.

Walking through the Cité de Carcassonne, it's impossible not to feel transported. Its turreted walls, grand gates, and medieval alleys seem to rise out of a dream. Yet, behind the romantic silhouette is a living city shaped by sieges, trade, faith, and resilience. From the Gothic towers of the Basilica of Saints Nazarius and Celsus to the majestic Château Comtal and the echoes of Cathar resistance,

Carcassonne is a living museum one that invites you not just to look, but to listen, explore, and imagine.

Beyond the fortress, the rhythm of daily life flows through the Bastide Saint-Louis, where locals gather in sun-drenched squares and friendly conversations fill open-air markets. The gentle glide of boats along the Canal du Midi, the scent of lavender and thyme on the breeze, the taste of cassoulet shared with a glass of local wine these are the sensory layers that make Carcassonne much more than its iconic silhouette.

What truly sets Carcassonne apart is its ability to make you feel part of something greater. It's a place where architecture and nature, history and hospitality, myth and modern life coexist effortlessly. You may arrive as a visitor, but you leave with a connection to the land, to the past, and to the people who keep its spirit alive.

As you continue your travels, let Carcassonne inspire you to seek depth in every destination. Let it remind you that sometimes the most memorable adventures are found in the quiet of ancient stones or the warmth of a shared meal. Whether you return someday to retrace your steps or share your stories with others, Carcassonne will linger with you a golden fortress in the mind, glowing at dusk, forever welcoming.

May your travels be filled with discovery, joy, and meaning and may Carcassonne remain a cherished chapter in your journey through the world.

Printed in Dunstable, United Kingdom